YOU CAN BE A FANTASTIC WORD OF MOUTH MARKETER!

You have something important to say about that thing you're so passionate about—your business, your cause, your art, your vision.

You want to spread your ideas to the ends of the earth. But, unfortunately, good ideas don't always get the recognition they deserve. You need to help them along, and that takes word of mouth marketing.

WHY YOU NEED THIS BOOK

You'll learn how to build an effective word of mouth marketing campaign that you can use to get people talking.

We're going to get specific: where to start, what to do, and how to make it successful.

You'll learn practical, how-to steps you can use right away—without a big budget.

WHY YOU NEED WORD OF MOUTH

Word of mouth marketing is the art of creating a company that people love to talk about. Now is the time to energize and inspire those fans who will talk about you because they love what you do.

You only have two ways to get your message out there: love or money.

You can buy advertising, which is paying people to talk about you. But you always pay, every time, forever.

When you earn word of mouth, people talk for love instead of money.

This book will help you become a great word of mouth marketer.

THE WORD OF MOUTH ON WORD OF MOUTH MARKETING

"A quick, practical, and extremely useful guide to word of mouth marketing."

— **Emanuel Rosen,**
author of *The Anatomy of Buzz*

"Great book on WOM. Nicely written."

— **Jack Trout,**
author of *Positioning: The Battle for Your Mind* and *The 22 Immutable Laws of Marketing*

"This book is to Gladwell's *The Tipping Point* as engineering is to physics. If you want to understand the deep sociological theories behind interpersonal communication, this isn't the book for you. If you want to understand how to harness interpersonal communication to drive your business, then buy this book."

— **David Godes, Associate Professor, Harvard Business School**

"Word of mouth is the valuable currency in today's advertising-saturated world. Andy Sernovitz has written a book packed with ideas on how to do word of mouth marketing the right way."

— **Jackie Huba and Ben McConnell, authors of *Creating Customer Evangelists***

"It's brief. It's elementary. It's obvious. But the truth often is. Read this book to relearn what you always knew just in time for it to change your business life."

— **Bob Garfield, co-host of NPR's *On The Media***

"Andy brings it together perfectly: the vision, the strategy, and the practical how-to. It's all here."

— **Geoff Ramsey, CEO, eMarketer**

"It's an actionable guide for anyone looking to capture the power of word of mouth. Andy has written a book that shows just how simple it is to get people talking about your business. You should read this book and then tell a friend."

— **Brad Santeler, Kimberly-Clark**

"A primer chock-full of great stories, tips, and exercises to make you a better word of mouth marketer, no matter what size company you work for. Read it, and you will increase your influence with your customers and make yourself more influential in your company."

— **Ed Keller and Jon Berry, authors of *The Influentials***

"It's easy to agree that word of mouth is important. But it's time to become students of how it works and why it is so valuable to our customers. Start or continue your journey by reading this book."

— **Bob Pearson, Dell**

"Andy's approach is practical, affordable, and, best of all, ethical. Don't waste your money on mass marketing: Spend it on this book and start people talking."

— **Greg Stielstra, author of *PyroMarketing***

"The coolest book on the hottest topic in marketing and communication. Andy tells it all and tells it like it really is. The Five Ts are the best organizing framework for word of mouth I have seen yet. Use them and profit. No hype. No smoke and mirrors. No overblown promises."

— **Don E. Schultz, Professor Emeritus-in-Service, Northwestern University**

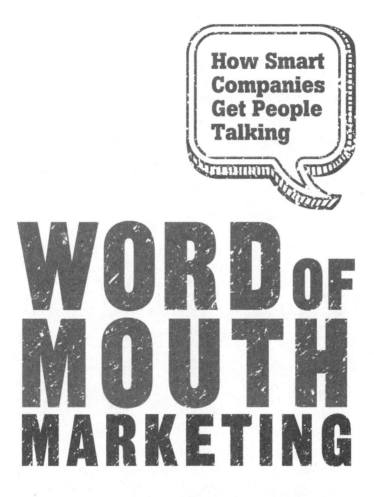

How Smart
Companies
Get People
Talking

WORD OF MOUTH MARKETING

Foreword by **Seth Godin** | Afterword by **Guy Kawasaki**

ANDY SERNOVITZ

PressBox
PUBLISHING

WORD OF MOUTH MARKETING
How Smart Companies Get People Talking

www.wordofmouthbook.com

Copyright © 2015 Andy Sernovitz.
All rights reserved.

ISBN: 978-0-9834290-3-6

Published by PressBox Publishing
3616 Far West Blvd., Suite 500
Austin, TX 78731
www.pressbox.org

Book design by TLC Graphics, *www.TLCGraphics.com*
Cover by Monica Thomas / Interior by Erin Stark

Cover photo credits: Old red pencil: ©iStockphoto.com/tap10 | Pen: ©Ingram Publishing Image Library | Colored pencil: ©Visual Symbols Library | Talk Bubble ©jammydesign | Tape: ©Roel Smart | Pencil: ©Martti Salmela

Publisher's Cataloging-In-Publication Data
(Prepared by The Donohue Group, Inc.)

The Library of Congress has cataloged the paperback edition as follows:

Sernovitz, Andy.
    Word of mouth marketing : how smart companies get people talking /
Andy Sernovitz ; foreword by Seth Godin ; afterword by Guy Kawasaki. – 3rd ed. p. ; cm.
    Includes bibliographical references.
    ISBN: 978-1-60832-366-1
    1. Word-of-mouth advertising. 2. Marketing. I. Godin, Seth. II. Kawasaki, Guy,
1954- III. Title.
HF5414 .S47 2012
658.87   2011943267

Printed in the United States of America

10 9 8 7 6 5 4

Fourth Edition

There is only one thing in the world worse than being talked about, and that is not being talked about.

— Oscar Wilde (*The Picture of Dorian Gray*)

CONTENTS

FOREWORD
BY SETH GODIN

People talk about Andy. Wherever he goes, whatever industry he's in, Andy Sernovitz causes a conversation.

That's his secret. Don't tell anyone (actually, go ahead—he won't mind). By causing a conversation, and then creating organizations that make it easy for the conversation to continue, Andy thrives. He is a living, breathing example of the power of word of mouth.

This isn't the first book on the topic (I wrote *Unleashing the Ideavirus* in 2000, and mine wasn't even the first). It probably won't be the last, either. But what this book offers you is two things: First, Andy's vision as honed through his work in the trenches, year after year. And second, an incredibly straightforward, jargon-free approach to a topic your boss keeps talking about. Be sure to show her the manifesto in chapter 3, which is worth the entire cost of the book.

Personally, I doubt whether anyone needs an association to dream up new ways to amplify word of mouth. What it does need, and what Andy's busy arguing for, is a group of people who keep pushing each other to do more and more remarkable stuff, to not settle, to create things that are actually worth talking about.

Have fun. Spread the word.

— **Seth Godin**
Author of *Unleashing the Ideavirus*

PREFACE

This is a book for everyone who has something to sell.

Word of mouth marketing isn't just for multinational corporations with huge marketing budgets. The ideas and practical information you'll find here will work just as well for a dry cleaner, a restaurant owner, or a dentist as they will for a Fortune 500 company. You don't need to be a marketing genius or an I-only-wear-black advertising guy.

Why? Because word of mouth marketing isn't about marketers or marketing. It's about real people and why those real people would want to talk about you and your stuff.

From here on out, I'll use the term *stuff* for *products and services*. Word of mouth marketing works for any kind of product or service. It also works for causes, ideas, charities, and organizations—anything that you want people to talk about.

I've been marketing for a long time, but I've never had a marketing budget. Despite that, I've sold a lot of stuff. Any success I've had has always been half creativity and half talking to a lot of people. I didn't know it at the time, but what I was doing then is what we now call *word of mouth marketing*—joining in the conversation that people are having every day with other people.

Good Marketing Is Easy

One of the most important things I've learned is that word of mouth marketing can be so easy and obvious that everyone misses just how easy and obvious it is. I get dozens of calls and emails every day from people asking how to get started. Small companies, big companies, everyone. There are a number of great books on the topic, but they are often specialized or theoretical. It seems there isn't a simple how-to-get-started-with-word-of-mouth book.

So here you go.

This book is full of inexpensive things that you can do today to get word of mouth started. There are tons of ideas here. You can start with steps as basic as a clever product name, a special service, a choice of uniform, a well-worded email, or being a little bit nicer to your customers.

People often say that I make marketing seem too simple.

I disagree. Marketing shouldn't be hard, and the best marketing never is.

This isn't a book about advanced techniques. You won't find any advice here that asks you to hire an agency or spend a lot of money. (I will mention some of the expensive-but-effective tactics just so you know what they are.) Many amazing agencies out there can help you create amazing word of mouth, and I recommend that you talk to them.

But this is a do-it-yourself book. This is what you can do on your own to get people talking about your company.

You'll do it well.

A Promise

When you are done with this book, you will be able to try one or two of the techniques I've talked about the next day, without spending more than $50 or a few hours of your time. The day after that, you'll have more people talking about your company. A week later, you'll have a lot more. Then you can dig in and really do it big.

INTRODUCTION

People love to talk.

People talk about products and services. People talk about hair color, cars, computers, sandwiches, TV shows, and floor cleaner. The stuff they use every day.

People are talking about you and what you sell right now. It might be a casual mention. It might be a scathing attack. It might be a scathing attack posted to Amazon, where 20 million people will read it before deciding whether to buy your stuff.

Or—it might be something really nice.

How much they love what you do. How their friends just have to try it. Why you are definitely better than the other guys. How wonderful it is to do business with you.

Maybe they'll say these nice things to their neighbors or write them on a blog, or review you on Amazon, where 20 million people will read it and decide to buy your stuff. This is, of course, what you'd like to have happen. And it's actually pretty easy to do.

Word of mouth marketing is about earning that good conversation.

It doesn't matter whether you're selling real estate, jelly, or jet engines. People will ask other people about you before they decide to buy from you. We turn to people we trust first—friends, family, coworkers, and other people like us—when starting to look for something to buy. Not ads, not brochures, not phone books.

So what is word of mouth marketing? In this book, I define it as, "Giving people a reason to talk about your stuff, and making it easier for that conversation to take place."

In the end, marketing is pretty easy: If people like your stuff, and if they trust you, they will tell their friends to do business with you.

Learn to make customers really, really happy. It doesn't take much more than that.

Understand this concept, devote yourself to it, and you will be a successful word of mouth marketer.

It's More than Just Marketing

This is nominally a book about a specific marketing technique. But it's really a new philosophy of business (and how to live it).

It's about honesty and admiration. It's about making people happy.

It's a simple philosophy, a new golden rule:

> ### Earn the respect and recommendation of your customers, and they will do the rest.
>
> - Treat people well, and they will do your marketing for you, for free.
>
> - Be interesting or be invisible.

When people trust you, they are willing to put their words on the line for you. Please them, inspire them, and they'll bring their friends to you.

What are your other options? Bore them—and be forced to spend millions in advertising to get them interested. Annoy them—and watch your customers walk away, taking their friends with them.

Advertising is the cost of being boring.

If your customers won't talk about your stuff, you have to pay newspapers and TV shows to do it for you. That's why you see lots of ads for cereal and toothpaste.

Word of mouth marketing is more than just marketing. It's about making your stuff and your company worth talking about.

How can you become buzzworthy?

Leveling the Playing Field

Word of mouth marketing works for any size business. You don't need to have a hot website, to be in a sexy industry, or to have a cool, innovative new technology. You can make it work if you're the one person who gets it inside a giant corporation. You can make it work for a single store with no advertising budget.

You just have to give people something to talk about.

I love Mario's Barbershop in Chicago. When I went in with my four-year-old son, they offered me a cocktail. They offered him a toy car. It's a guy place. No one ever accepts their drinks, but it's a blast to hang out with Mario, Zoran, and Bobby.

Those drinks are a reason to talk. I tell the other dads at day care. It comes up at parties. It's the first thing that comes to mind when someone mentions a haircut.

The result: a line of dads and kids out the door every Saturday. (A Supercuts on the same block is deserted.)

When I was single, there was no better date restaurant than Otello's in Washington, D.C. When I showed up with a woman, the owner would come out before the meal with a big, "It is soooo good to see you again. We are soooo happy you are here." (Of course, he had no idea who I was.) After dinner, he'd produce two glasses of cheap wine, on the house. This guy knew how to make sure you looked like a high roller.

You can only guess how many word of mouth recommendations he got.

There are hundreds of examples of simple ways to get people talking (most don't involve liquor).

Seth Godin calls it being "remarkable" in his book *Purple Cow*. *Remarkable* means worth remarking on, worth saying something about. It's the root concept of word of mouth marketing.

It's Not About the Internet

One of the great misconceptions about word of mouth marketing is that it's all happening online. The role of the internet and the new ways people use it to communicate are indisputably critical components of the sudden spread of word of mouth. Blogs and social media are a big deal because they empower lots of people to share ideas.

But that's only a part of it—only about 20 percent of word of mouth happens online. When it does play a role, it usually sparks the 80 percent of word of mouth conversations that actually happen face-to-face.

So let me apologize up front. A lot of the examples I use are about things you can do with the internet. These stories tend to make good examples. I talk about blogs and online communities because the word of mouth you find there is very visible—it's written down publicly for everyone to see. Many of the recommendations you'll read involve things you can do online, because it's the easiest way to reach people. But word of mouth is not just about the internet and not just for online businesses.

Real word of mouth dips in and out of different spaces. You eat at a good restaurant. You mention it to people at the office. One of them emails your recommendation to his wife. She emails four friends, and they have lunch there. Two mention the restaurant to other friends at a party, and one of them blogs about it. Someone reads the blog and calls a buddy about eating there. They review it online. You get the idea.

Word of Mouth Marketing Makes Us More Honest

Now, here's where it gets interesting. Word of mouth marketing only works if you have good products and services. It only works if people like you and trust you. (If you're a jerk, word of mouth will backfire horribly on you.)

If your product or service sucks, no PR campaign, clever TV ad, or announcement on your website will make consumers believe that it doesn't. Not anymore. And the speed of word of mouth on the internet spreads the truth almost instantly.

You don't hear a lot of good word of mouth about cable companies.

When word of mouth works, good companies are rewarded with gobs of free advertising and attention, and they make more money.

When word of mouth works *better*, bad products and bad companies are punished with negative buzz, and they lose customers.

Think about what this means for you and your family. We have a new social force that rewards companies with free marketing, sales, and profits when they treat people well and produce good products. The same force stops companies from treating people badly by killing their sales.

For the first time in the history of modern business, we have a *force for good* that is also driven by the *all-powerful profit motive*. For years, government regulators and consumer advocates have tried to use legal and public pressure to make companies treat people well. I'll bet that the profit motive works better.

This is why word of mouth marketing is so exciting. Everyone can do it. It makes money. It makes products and services better. It makes business more honest and ethical.

It's good for all of us.

Everyone Is Already Talking About You

So here's the deal: You're getting talked about whether you like it or not. The conversation has started, so you might as well get involved.

A lot of that talk is happening online. Millions of people blog, millions more post online reviews, and everyone Googles you.

But even more is happening offline—as it always has. Each and every one of us talks to a friend or family member before we buy something. We listen to our friends before we bother going to a store or restaurant. And we don't just ask for advice—we also make recommendations about what we liked and what we hated.

So what about the negative? What if people say bad things about you? Too late—if it's going to happen, it's going to happen. Unless you're the perfect company, it probably already has.

So you only have two choices: let people talk about you, spread rumors, and get it wrong; or join in, participate, and make it work for you.

Advertising is the cost of being boring.

Yes, it's uncomfortable. The first time you search the blogs for your product name, it's usually a real surprise—sort of like walking into a crowded party when the laughter suddenly stops and everyone looks at you.

But it's different. Because everyone is waiting for you to join the conversation. The door is open, everyone is listening, and they want you to be a part of it. So jump in.

The best part is, the more you participate, the more the conversation grows, and the more it is about you. Feed it, put the good stuff out there, and the conversation will be dynamic and positive. That's what this book is about—learning the right way to participate and make the most of this wonderful opportunity.

A NOTE TO THE READER

How to Get Started

Read this book.

Then try a few of the simple suggestions. People will start talking about you in just a few days.

Then do a few of the more involved ideas. Even more people will start talking about you.

And when you have a chance, think about the philosophy behind word of mouth marketing (called *Deep Stuff* in chapter 2). This is a little bit more complicated and not as immediate, but more important.

When these ideas jell, everyone will be talking about you, they will respect your company. And they will like you better. And you'll like you and your company better, too.

And that is very cool.

Examples, Stories, and Data

This book is full of anecdotes, stories, and examples. They are true but not always verifiable. I heard many of them through word of mouth.

Also, you'll find almost no hard data, numbers, or statistics. This was an intentional choice.

Many great books and resources provide detailed analysis and data about the phenomena and trends discussed here. Also, a robust word of mouth research industry produces immense amounts of very useful data.

For our purposes in this book, however, it doesn't really matter. The point is to share examples that help you understand the magic of word of mouth and stories that show how you can use it for yourself. The specifics aren't as important as the lessons.

This book is about simple, actionable things you can do. It's not a business case study or a textbook. It's the story of a new kind of marketing that is easier, more effective, and more accessible to the average businessperson. The numbers sometimes get in the way of telling that story.

The Great Word of Mouth Hyphen Controversy

A brief aside for all the editors and strict grammarians reading this: Yes, I do know that *word of mouth* is often hyphenated as *word-of-mouth*. Actually, it's only supposed to be hyphenated when it's an adjective—"word-of-mouth marketing"—and not when it's a noun. But no one ever gets it right, so I'm going to skip the hyphens. That's the advantage of being one of the first people in a new industry—you get to define the terms.

Now that this is written, I am allowed to return home to my wife, the professional editor, who still isn't happy about all of this. But I hope she will settle for this note, as she graciously accepts many far worse quirks.

More Great Stuff

We've got a whole website that goes with this book. Check it out at *www.wordofmouthbook.com*. That's where you can download the worksheets from this book and find a bunch of other useful tools.

And if you like the ideas in this book, be sure to check out *www.wordofmouth.org* where every day we share great ideas on how to get more people talking about you. It's full of downloads, videos, worksheets, newsletters—everything you'd ever want to know about being a great word of mouth marketer.

Finally, check out my blog, "Damn, I Wish I'd Thought of That!" at *www.damniwish.com*. I share a lot of unusually useful ideas for smart marketers and resources to help you master word of mouth. It's also where I test and demonstrate a lot of the ideas that you'll read here.

THE ESSENTIAL CONCEPTS

WHAT IS WORD OF MOUTH MARKETING?

Get People Talking

Here's the definition of word of mouth marketing:

1. Giving people a reason to talk about your stuff
2. Making it easier for that conversation to take place

Even simpler: It's everything you can do to get people talking.

If you like acronyms, think of it this way: Word of mouth marketing is "CtoC" marketing. You've heard about business-to-business (BtoB) and business-to-consumer (BtoC) marketing. Word of mouth marketing is about real people talking to each other—consumer to consumer (CtoC)—instead of marketers doing the talking.

Actually, it's BtoCtoC. Your job as a marketer is to put out an idea worth talking about. That's marketing. When a real person repeats it, that's word of mouth. It's about the second hop (and the third hop, and the fourth hop, and so on).

Right after our son was born, my wife and I saw an ad for a weekly show at our local movie theater where you were encouraged to bring infants. Now featuring screaming and pooping right in the theater! What a great idea! Any parent of a newborn knows that you probably won't see another movie together until the kid gets old enough to be embarrassed to be seen with you.

What was the first thing we did? We called every other parent in our apartment building and brought them with us. The promotion that we saw was traditional marketing. The 12 conversations we had with other parents was word of mouth marketing at its best.

It's All About the Second M

Word of mouth has been with us forever. What's new is the second M—marketing.

Word of mouth exists. Word of mouth *marketing* is working with it toward a marketing objective. Word of mouth *marketing* is a new specialty that is as actionable, trackable, and planable as any other form of marketing.

Word of mouth is natural conversation between real people. Word of mouth *marketing* is working within this conversation so people are talking about you.

Word of mouth is about genuine consumer conversations. Word of mouth *marketing* is joining that conversation and participating in it—but never, ever manipulating, faking, or degrading its fundamental honesty in any way.

Why Now?

If word of mouth has been around forever, there must be some reason why marketers suddenly began talking about it.

Here's what's new: We can finally do something about it.

It's evolved from *anecdotal* to *actionable*, from something that just happens to something you can influence. Word of mouth marketing has become the fastest growing form of marketing because we now have the tools and knowledge to work with it.

Until a few years ago, we sort of wished that good word of mouth would just happen on its own. You could have a special sale or do some silly publicity stunt and hope people would talk.

Now we can work with people who want to talk about us and help their ideas reach a new audience. We can provide a platform so more people hear what our fans are saying. We can use the internet to give far more visibility to a conversation that has always been happening.

We've also gained the ability to track and measure that conversation. Thanks in part to blogs and the web, we can see who is saying what about us. We can listen to the conversation and understand it. We can figure out who is talking and why they are talking. It's not such a mystery anymore.

Family legend has it that my grandfather Gene was the first person to hire a teenage Elvis Presley to perform in public. At the department store where he worked in Memphis, he had this unknown kid play his guitar from the back of a truck in the parking lot. I'm sure it got some people talking, but it wasn't a big deal at the time.

These days, we'd do it a little differently. We'd announce the concert on the web. We'd email a note to people who blog about the local music scene. We'd give flyers to kids at local high schools and invite them to a free show. We'd put the invitation in an email so it could get easily forwarded. We'd try to hire a band with a big social media following, so it could get its fans to show up. We'd use all those cheap and easy things that get lots of people talking.

Later, I'll go into detail on these techniques and explain how to make them work for you.

It's More than Marketing (or Maybe Not Marketing at All)

In many cases, word of mouth marketing isn't actually about marketing at all. It's about great customer service that makes people want to tell their friends about you. It's about fantastic products that people can't resist showing to everyone.

This is called *organic* word of mouth—word of mouth that springs naturally from the positive qualities of your company. Many experts would argue that this is the only legitimate form of word of mouth. The opposite concept is called *amplified* word of mouth—word of mouth that is started by an intentional campaign to get people talking. I like the organic kind better, but we'll learn about both.

I like the idea that consumers reward companies that have earned their respect with great word of mouth. Nothing beats coming up with a product so interesting that people just can't help talking about it. Nothing is better than customers taking it upon themselves to support a business that they love.

TiVo is the classic example. They aren't known for their advertising. In fact, TiVo has hardly advertised at all. But everyone knows what TiVo is.

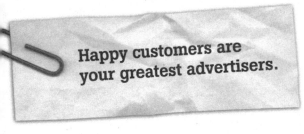

Happy customers are your greatest advertisers.

TiVo owners are maniacs. They absolutely will not stop talking about their TiVos. They will chase you down and drag you to their living rooms to make you see a demonstration. Their love for the product turns them into crazy, passionate word of mouth promoters.

You see the same passion from people who love OXO utensils, Aeron chairs, or Camper shoes. You see it from Yankees fans and teenagers in love with rock bands.

Organic word of mouth is created by products that get your customers to love you so much that they just can't shut up.

And sometimes the best word of mouth is exceptional customer service—think of the famously generous return policies of Nordstrom or the fact that Enterprise Rent-A-Car will pick you up at home.

I pay a little more than I should to do business with my cell phone company and my web hosting company, because they answer my calls on the first ring, and they usually solve my problems on the first call. Of course, I also tell everyone who asks that they'd be crazy to work with anyone else.

There's a great little conference call service in Fairfield, Iowa, called Conference Calls Unlimited. Pretty much all conference call services look the same and do the same thing, so it's difficult to stand out from the crowd. It's a boring business, and advertising is expensive and ineffective when you sell the same thing as everyone else.

So what did they do? They stopped advertising. They put everything they had into customer service. These guys will do anything for you. They take care of their customers, whatever it takes. It's surprisingly pleasant and interesting to work with them, despite the uninteresting nature of what they sell.

As you can imagine, the word of mouth they get is fantastic. This isn't the first book to mention this tiny company.

Traditional marketing is no longer the safe way to go. It may make you more comfortable, but it is becoming gradually less and less effective for more and more companies. It's time to focus on making customers happy—earning their trust and respect and getting them talking about your stuff.

The Four Rules
of Word of Mouth Marketing

Rule #1: Be Interesting

Nobody talks about boring companies, boring products, or boring ads. If you want people to talk about you, you've got to do something special. Anything. If you are boring, you'll never get a moment of conversation. Your word of mouth will fall flat on its face. (Actually, it will just fade away, unnoticed.)

Before you run an ad, before you launch a product, before you put something new on the menu, ask the magic question: Would anyone tell a friend about this?

Take a trick from the Chicago Bagel Authority's 56 bizarrely named sandwiches, like the Hoosier Daddy and the Muenster Mash. Or the seven-inch-high corned beef sandwiches at New York's famous Carnegie Deli. It would still be the best corned beef sandwich in the world if it were a normal size. But its insane mass guarantees that hundreds of tourists leave the restaurant every day to spread the word about one of the greatest sights in the Big Apple.

There are probably hundreds of shoeshine stands in New York City. But everybody goes to Eddie's in Grand Central Station. They tell their friends to make a special trip to go there (passing plenty of other good shoeshine stands on the way). Why? Eddie's has huge, comfy, old-fashioned, red leather easy chairs to sit in. You feel like a king when you sit back and enjoy a few minutes of peace in those chairs at the end of the day.

Give people a reason to talk about you.

And please, I beg you, stop for a minute before you buy more advertising. Think about how much money you are about to spend. Think about how fast you, and everyone else in the world, flip past hundreds of ads without even noticing them.

Don't run another ad unless it is truly worth talking about.

Rule #2: Make It Easy

Word of mouth is lazy. You've got to help it along if you expect it to go anywhere.

You need to do two things: Find a super-simple message and help people share it.

Start with a topic that anyone can remember. Something like, "Our software doesn't crash," or, "They have chocolate cream cheese!" or, "They give you snacks while you're waiting for a table," or, "Stupid name, but it sure does work." (Anything longer than a sentence is too much. It'll get forgotten or mangled.)

We all think of Steve Jobs as the greatest computer marketer who ever lived. So what did he do when he returned to Apple in 1996 with the mission of reviving a stumbling company? Did he talk about great software? Stable operating systems? No.

Jobs's great marketing insight was … pink and purple computers.

It got everyone talking. It restarted positive word of mouth about the company. Everyone told a friend, because they had a simple topic of conversation that was interesting to share. And when people heard about the cute computers, they were ready to take another look at the more important features.

Once you've got your big word of mouth idea, find a bunch of ways to make it easier to spread. There are countless easy ways to make your ideas portable. A special announcement on a website or brochure is stuck in place. But when you put it in an email or post it to a social network, it's in motion.

Rule #3: Make People Happy

Happy customers are your greatest advertisers.

Thrill them. Create amazing products. Provide excellent service. Go the extra mile. Make the experience remarkable. Fix problems. Make sure the work you do gets people energized, excited, and eager to tell a friend.

When people like you, they share you with their friends. They want to help you, they want to support your business, and they want their friends to enjoy what you offer. You will get more word of mouth from making people happy than anything else you could possibly do.

Let's look at one of the great mysteries of the modern age. In 1999, why did 60,000 people drive their plain Saturn sedans to Spring Hill, Tennessee, to meet the people who made them? What car could possibly be less interesting than a Saturn?

The annual Saturn Homecoming was a great word of mouth marketing strategy. But it wouldn't have worked if people didn't trust and respect Saturn. People really liked the company. They liked its attitude. They felt taken care of by the nice salespeople and the company's no-haggle concept. They were amazed when they got a friendly note twice a year with instructions on how to adjust the clock for daylight saving time.

So they told their friends. They supported the company that supported them.

Let's look at another great mystery of the modern age. Why do some people like Target so much? This I won't attempt to explain, but I'm not the only guy who, while on vacation, has been taken to visit a Target *that looks exactly like the one we have at home*. (Aargh.) But they have some stylish stuff. Decent prices. Clean stores. A fun attitude.

Target makes my wife happy in a way that would threaten a less manly man.

And she talks to everyone about it.

Rule #4: Earn Trust and Respect

If you don't have respect, you don't get good word of mouth.

Nobody talks positively about a company that they don't trust or like. Nobody puts their name on the line for a company that will embarrass them in front of their friends.

Always be an honorable company. Make ethics part of everything you do. Be good to your customers. Talk to them. Fulfill their needs.

Make people proud to tell your story to everyone they know.

Southwest Airlines is one of the most trusted brands in the world. It treats its customers well, with few hassles and a great attitude. It treats its employees well, with stable jobs, a no-lay-off policy, and decent pay. People like Southwest. People like the company so much that they sent cash to the airline after 9/11 to help it out.

> If you don't have respect, you don't get good word of mouth.

Lots of people are spreading great word of mouth about Southwest. Does anyone have anything good to say about most other airlines?

Every company can be nicer, and every employee can work to make his or her company a little better to its customers.

My bank offers pretty much the same services as every other bank. But they are really nice. Really, really nice. Tom and Abby remember my name and my wife's name. They even remember my baby's name, and she doesn't do much banking.

I banked at one of the top three banks for ten years, and at one time my company had more than $1 million on deposit. I could barely get them to cash a check or take my calls. And after a while, the random, punitive fees started to eat away any respect I had for this venerable institution. Negative word of mouth from people like me has sent a whole lot of money to banks that treat people better.

The Three Reasons
People Talk About You

You won't get good at word of mouth marketing until you really understand what motivates people to talk about the stuff they talk about.

People love to talk and share opinions. They love to talk about people and ideas. They love to talk about stuff to buy, from the sexy and fun to the dull and mundane.

Three basic motivations drive word of mouth conversations.

The Three Reasons People Talk About You		
YOU	**ME**	**US**
It's about the stuff: the company and products	It's about the talker: making them feel good	It's about the group: feeling connected
• They love you (and your stuff). • They hate you. • You've given them something to talk about. • You've made it easy for them to talk about you.	• They feel smart. • They feel important. • They want to help people. • They want to express themselves.	• They are part of the brand family. • They belong to a community. • They are part of a team.

Reason #1: You—They Like You and Your Stuff

People talk because you're doing or selling something that they want to talk about. They love your products. They like how you treat them. You've done something interesting.

It's about giving them a reason to talk about you. The more interesting you get, the more motivated the talkers are. Your customers aren't going to love or hate you (or feel indifferent to you) for no reason.

Bottom line: You've got to arouse some passion before your advocates will begin talking about your company. If you've given them something to love, you can build on that. If you've given them something to hate or ignore, you'll have to address that before you can worry about the rest.

A decent product gets recommended to a friend, but only passively—usually when they are asked directly about it:

"What kind of grill should I buy?"

"I've got a Weber; it's pretty good."

You get much more word of mouth when you make your products worth talking about. The more you make your product buzzworthy, the more it pushes itself into the conversation. The special satisfaction that people get from something great is what moves them from being a passive recommender to an active one:

"Check this out. My new grill has a Pork-A-Licious Thingamabob. You've got to try it!"

Being worth talking about doesn't mean being complicated or expensive. Let's look at a $2 pen, the Zebra F-301. I mean, what is there to talk about, really? A pen is a pen. It has ink, and it writes. What's the big deal?

Well, it turns out that it's a pretty good pen. No radical leap forward in pen technology, just a cool-looking, stainless-steel, smooth-writing pen that people want to talk about. It's so good that it has inspired actual fans, as well as a huge amount of word of mouth. These fans write hundreds of product reviews and blog posts raving about … a $2 pen.

Giving people something to talk about means being creative with how you present your products, services, and company. The day-to-day existence of your business doesn't provide a reason to talk. You've got to keep putting new topics out there.

Even your most die-hard fans need something new to keep them interested on an ongoing basis. Without that extra oomph, you don't have a conversation. But when you do something special, your fans go bonkers.

We all love White Castle (in that Rolaids kind of way). And White Castle gets decent word of mouth. People talk about it, even make movies about it. But it's not a part of our day-to-day conversation. So what did White Castle do? It announced that you could make reservations at White Castle on Valentine's Day. What a silly idea. What a wacky dinner date. What a great reason to talk.

You don't need to be that clever. You just need to keep it fresh. If nothing special is happening at your business, there is no reason for anyone to talk about you. Find something. Do a promotion, publish a report, have a sale, stock a new line of products. Anything.

What makes your product worth talking about?

Reason #2: Me—Talking Makes Me Feel Good

Word of mouth often comes down to emotion more than products or product features. We're driven to share by feelings that are far more about us as individuals than about what a business is doing.

The emotions that drive us to talk aren't complicated.

We want to look smart

A lot of people get their kicks out of being the expert on their favorite subject. When we tell people about what to buy, we're showing off what we know. Some people do this really well, and everyone goes to them for advice. We love to talk to these people when we're making a purchase, and they love to tell us what they think.

With blogs and online communities, it's gone to a whole new level. People put up pages where they can show off and share. It becomes a labor of love. You also see these people on message boards, those die-hard volunteers who answer everyone else's questions. They are out there as the expert for everyone to see.

Help these people look smarter. Give them newsletters, inside information, technical detail. More is better. They'll love you for it.

We want to help other people

The desire to look smart is often paired with a higher-level motivation: to help other people. Some people are so passionate about what they know that they want everyone else to enjoy what they are enjoying. It bugs them to see someone buy the wrong brand or get stuck with an inferior product.

These are the folks who come up to you in a store when you're trying to decide what to buy and give you an unprompted sales pitch for what they think is the greatest product in the world. Annoying, yes, but driven by a genuine desire to help you out.

Ever met a Macintosh groupie? How could you not? A certain kind of Mac user is so emotionally connected to the brand that they want everyone else to use it. They believe it will surely make everyone's life easier—and possibly cause peace on earth.

Help these folks help others: Give them samples to share, flyers to distribute, and messages to forward.

We want to feel important

Some people talk because they like being asked. They get a kick out of being the expert. The more people ask for their advice, the more important they feel. It feels good to be an authority figure.

Find ways to recognize these customers and give them higher status simply by acknowledging them, keeping them in the loop, and asking for their input. Being a frequent flyer used to be as much about the gold luggage tag as the miles and rewards.

These customers will talk about you and your stuff because it shows off their importance and expertise and because they feel like they're in the inner circle.

Give them things that make them feel important: special status, private shopping hours, or advance news.

Reason #3: Us—We Feel Connected to the Group

The desire to be a part of a group is one of the most powerful human emotions. We want very badly to be connected.

Talking about products is one way we achieve that connection. Our jeans, our cars, where we shop, and the beer we drink all are ways we show who we are.

We are emotionally rewarded when we share excitement with a group that has a common interest. We share a bond with people who like the same teams or bands that we do, and we feel a similar connection with those who like the same cars or clothes. The passion generated by being in a group of enthusiasts translates very easily into word of mouth.

Members of groups that coalesce around specific brands, such as Harley-Davidson riders, Macintosh users, and Nikon owners, are the most likely to talk about the companies' products.

Working with this motivation is all about group recognition. It's giving away T-shirts, hats, bumper stickers, or temporary tattoos. It's holding events and rallies that bring people together.

You've got to make these people feel special, like part of the family, as though they have some skin in the game.

How to Stop Word of Mouth

Prizes and Rewards

Mixing love and money is usually a bad idea.

Offering customers incentives to spread the word about your stuff is often a mistake. Here's why: You make them feel dirty if they're paid for it. Some things just shouldn't be for sale—friendship, certain kinds of favors, and your recommendation.

People are engaging in word of mouth because they love you or it makes them feel good. When you offer a monetary reward (or discounts, points, or miles) for a referral, you make it awkward and creepy.

Just at the moment someone is about to recommend you, they think, "If my friend finds out I'm being paid for this, they're not going to trust me. I'd better not say anything."

Even worse, incentives and rewards often create negative word of mouth. When you pay for it, you risk having people say, "This product is so bad, they need to *pay* people to talk about it."

The very powerful emotions that create word of mouth and the resulting affinity with your brand are nothing to be trifled with. You can deeply insult a loyal talker by offering to pay them for doing it.

Like everything in word of mouth marketing, these ideas are plenty obvious when you think about them. But you'll soon realize that these obvious ideas turn out to be the opposite of what traditional marketing teaches us to do.

A lot of companies offer their current customers rewards for signing up their friends. Whenever I get one of these emails or cards from a friend, I always think, "Well, that's great. You get $50. But what's in it for me?" It turns the friend-to-friend relationship into a salesperson-to-prospect transaction. Even good friends or family members are less believable when they're working for rewards.

But do you remember the original MCI Friends and Family promotion? It was all about mutual benefit. When you told a friend about the program, each of you got a reduced phone bill. You both benefited, equally and together. It kept the motives pure, it respected altruism, and everyone felt good about it. It was all about sharing the savings, not one person making money off the other. It's still one of the greatest word of mouth programs in history.

Overexposure

When you understand why people talk, one more lesson is clear: Overexposure kills word of mouth.

When everyone knows about something, no one needs to talk about it. Nothing could be dorkier than saying, "Hey, have you heard about *Star Wars*?" There's an obvious but often overlooked aspect to word of mouth—it is inspired and kept going by newness. When inline skates and Sony Walkmans were new, they were on everyone's lips. Twenty years later, they're not so remarkable.

Forgetting Why People Talk About You

Krispy Kreme was built on word of mouth. Then they killed the conversation with overexposure.

Remember when those were the most special doughnuts on planet Earth? Krispy Kreme had an amazing word of mouth topic—hot, gooey doughnuts. And there was a big neon sign that lit up—"HOT NOW"—when fresh doughnuts were coming off the line.

If you lived in a town with a Krispy Kreme, it was an event, even a tourist destination. You did silly things to show it off. When my wife visited a college friend in Toledo, they went on a mission to get those doughnuts at the instant of freshness. There were two stores about a mile apart. They actually drove back and forth between the stores until the light came on and they could dash in to get those hot doughnuts.

Everyone, and I mean everyone, was talking about those doughnuts. The word of mouth gods smiled upon them and their sugary goodness.

Then the company tried to make Krispy Kreme as common as Dunkin' Donuts. What built the chain's great word of mouth—the fact that the doughnuts were hard to get, fresh, and in limited supply—disappeared when Krispy Kreme put its pastries, cold and stiff, on every store shelf. This sudden and massive overexposure killed what was special—in other words, what was buzzworthy or remarkable.

Nobody tells their friends about food you can buy in a gas station.

The Five Ts of Word of Mouth Marketing

Sometimes great word of mouth is an accident. Sometimes it's a well-planned campaign. Either way, certain basic elements need to be in place for word of mouth to spread like crazy.

These elements are the Five Ts: Talkers, Topics, Tools, Taking Part, and Tracking.

1. *Talkers:* Who will tell their friends about you?

2. *Topics:* What will they talk about?

3. *Tools:* How can you help the message travel?

4. *Taking Part:* How should you join the conversation?

5. *Tracking:* What are people saying about you?

I've studied hundreds of great word of mouth successes. Every single one has the Five Ts, whether it's a big business or a small business, a Silicon Valley wonder or business-to-business manufacturer, a national chain or a single restaurant.

Each time you start a word of mouth campaign, take a few minutes to go through these five steps and figure out how they fit into what you're selling. The process is simpler than you think, and it will guarantee that you'll create effective word of mouth marketing.

1. Talkers—Find People Who Will Talk About You

Talkers are any group of people who have the enthusiasm and connections to relay your message. Sometimes they are called "influencers" or "evangelists"—but don't let these terms make it sound as though you need some exotic system to find them.

Talkers are regular people. Talkers are your customers, your doctor, your neighbors, your friends.

Sometimes they are new customers bubbling with enthusiasm; sometimes they are rabid fans who volunteer to spread your message. They may be part of a formal word of mouth program, or they may be bloggers who happen to cover your topic.

We all know some talkers. There's the neighbor everyone goes to for advice on travel, the friend who knows every doctor in town, and the coworker who always knows about the best happy hour. Every product has some talkers—and you're probably the talker for something. (What do people ask you about?)

Talkers talk because they love to share great ideas and help their friends. They'll talk about you if you give them something to talk about and if they like you. It doesn't take much more than that.

Don't confuse talkers with trendsetters, celebrities, or journalists. Bellhops, cabbies, and office computer gurus do far more talking, day after day.

The people who will talk about your stuff are closer than you think. Your best talkers are probably customers you interact with every day who would love to be given the opportunity to do a little more.

Think about the fans of a rock band. They spend hundreds of dollars to support and promote a band they love, and they insist that their friends do the same. They *want* to spread the word and will even pay (through purchases of music, concert tickets, T-shirts, and posters) to do it.

Once you identify the right group of talkers, your next challenge is to give them a topic that they are willing to talk about.

2. Topics—Give People a Reason to Talk

All word of mouth starts with creating a message that will spread.

It doesn't need to be fancy. A special sale, remarkably good service, a cool new feature, a unique flavor, a funny name, or a nice package may be all it takes. The specifics of the message don't matter.

Good topics are portable, clear ideas that one person can repeat successfully.

Commerce Bank was a very friendly, helpful bank with the motto "America's Most Convenient Bank." Sort of generic. But their word of mouth topic? A free change-counting machine in the lobby called the Penny Arcade. Everyone talked about the only bank around that would let anyone (even noncustomers) turn change into bills, when most banks won't do it at all.

JetBlue created an amazing topic with their onboard TVs. Now, these TVs are nothing special. (Trust me, basic cable at 30,000 feet is still infomercials and reruns of *Saved by the Bell*.) But it's an easy idea to share. It's easy to repeat. It reminds people of the airline and starts them thinking about the other positive qualities of the brand. No one will tell a friend about the "low-cost, high-personality service model with an efficient structure and dedication to customers that results in quality service." But they will say, "Hey, JetBlue has TV!"

People share surprisingly simple and stupid things. Take a moment and look at your inbox. What have your friends sent you? Jokes, videos, and coupons.

Once you find a topic that is interesting enough to motivate your talkers, your next challenge is to give them tools to help encourage that conversation.

3. Tools—Help the Message Spread Faster and Farther

Even the best topics need a little help to spread.

Word of mouth marketers make their biggest impact when they provide the infrastructure to help messages travel. The recent growth of word of mouth as a marketing technique is largely due to the growth of the tools that we have to support conversations that are already happening.

Provide the tools that help your messages move farther and faster. An easy-to-forward email and a tell-a-friend button on the product page of your website are two incredibly powerful (but simple) online examples.

If you run a store or restaurant, don't let someone walk out the door without something to give to a friend, like a menu or a coupon.

Kiehl's cosmetics stores are famous for their free samples. It's impossible to leave without a pocket full of goodies. And they always give you more than one, so you have something to share with a friend.

If someone's got a desire to talk about you, do everything possible to help them along.

Magazines figured this out a long time ago. Although it seems over the top, there is a reason why every magazine has a flurry of subscription postcards falling all over your house. People share magazines, and those cards are the tools that help pass along the subscription offer.

A special sale or unique product (the topic) may be worth talking about, but it has exponential marketing power when you pack it into an easy-to-forward email (the tool). A blog is a tool that enables a company to talk directly with fans, giving them a story to share. Online communities create a home and a focus for otherwise disparate conversations. Formal evangelism programs provide the support and encouragement that keep fans talking.

Once you've created tools to accelerate the word of mouth, your next challenge is to keep that conversation fresh and fast-moving by taking part in it.

4. Taking Part—Join the Conversation

The idea of taking part gives marketers the heebie-jeebies.

Once you open the door to word of mouth conversations, there's no way to shut it again. When you reach out to real people and encourage them to start talking about your brand, they expect you to participate.

When people are talking about you, answer them. Reply to email messages, accept comments on your blog, participate in the discussion board, answer the phone. Thank bloggers who write about you. If you come across complaints, find out why the conversation is negative and fix it. Be helpful. Be truthful. Be thankful. Be nice.

If you don't join the conversation, it will die out. (Or turn against you if you are seen as aloof.)

Yes, it can be scary, especially at first. You'll get negative feedback, you'll even get crackpots, and you'll need to assign staff to listen to and learn from the conversation. At the same time, however, you'll be earning the respect and recommendations of your customers and building powerful long-term relationships.

Once you are a part of the dialogue, your next challenge is to track the conversation and learn what people are talking about.

5. Tracking—Measure and Understand What People Are Saying

Amazing tools have been developed that enable us to understand how word of mouth conversations travel and to follow what consumers are saying about us.

Tracking what is being said about you and your company is now a whole lot easier. You can find every comment about you on every blog and message board, moments after they are written. A deep understanding of the word of mouth being spread about you is now at your fingertips, instantly, for free.

Thanks to the popularity of blogs and online communities, people are now writing down every fleeting thought and publishing them online. ("I ate a sandwich. It was tasty. Do you like sandwiches? Comment on my blog!")

Because they are written down, these consumer-to-consumer conversations are easy to find and to measure—a major knowledge boon for marketers. Monitoring online communication lets you understand what consumers really think about your brand, your marketing, and your products. It provides a level of genuine understanding that is more authentic and immediate than the data from traditional research techniques.

Your next challenge is to learn to value this raw consumer word of mouth and to use it to build a smarter marketing plan and a better company.

Case Study:
Intuit—
Using the Five Ts

Let's look at a product with great word of mouth: QuickBooks. Software for small business bookkeeping is never fun, but Intuit masterfully uses the Five Ts to keep the word of mouth conversation going.

- Accountants are usually the first to recommend an accounting product. But Intuit realized that they had another great group of *Talkers*: small business owners who answer each others' questions about bookkeeping. Plumbers, graphic designers, hair stylists (you know, regular people) were helping their friends with the day-to-day challenges of running a small business by talking about products.

- The *Topic* evolved directly from the talkers. People were telling their friends, "You're not alone; there is a community who will help you with your bookkeeping questions."

- The *Tool* Intuit uses is a website called Intuit Community. It's a place where users—and future customers—can find people like themselves and talk about bookkeeping. A plumber with his own business can join a conversation with people just like him. The website facilitates the conversation among these regular people who learn from one another's experience and pass along helpful information about the product. What might have been a private conversation between two buddies is now shared publicly, viewable by millions of potential customers.

- Intuit *Takes Part* by joining in the conversation. All sorts of Intuit employees are encouraged to answer questions, share ideas, solve problems, and be part of the community. In a world where many software companies barely answer the phone, this participation earns them incredible respect—and more word of mouth.

- Finally, Intuit *Tracks* the word of mouth with detailed record-keeping and ongoing surveys. They use the word of mouth discussion to learn what works, where there are problems, how to improve the software, and how to keep customers happy.

Word of Mouth Marketing Isn't Deception

Listen closely: Deception, infiltration, dishonesty, and any attempt to manipulate consumers or the conversation are morally bankrupt practices. Plus, they just don't work in the long run.

Honest marketers do not do this and will not do this.

Dishonest marketers will get caught if they try. Sleazy behavior will be exposed by the public, who will turn on anyone who attempts it.

Word of mouth marketing is not what is known as *stealth marketing*: lying to people or shilling (a marketer pretending to be a regular customer to promote a product). It's not going into chat rooms with fake identities. It's not posting fake positive reviews on websites. It's not sending employees out to bars disguised as eager fans.

Honest marketers oppose all forms of stealth and deception.

Word of mouth marketing is about listening to consumers and giving them a voice. Stealth marketing is tricking people. You don't get good customers by lying to them.

If you're being sneaky or deceptive, you will get busted. Consumers today are incredibly savvy and independent, with the information and resources to catch you in a lie and tell everyone about it. The power of the consumer voice will make dishonest companies pay a steep price.

Word of Mouth Can't Be Faked

Word of mouth marketing can only succeed when people trust each other to talk honestly about what they like and don't like.

You cannot fake word of mouth. It just doesn't work without the trust. You might be able to fool a few people for a little while. But in the end, people will figure out that you faked it. Then you get embarrassed, you make enemies, and you lose sales.

Let's say a restaurant posts fake reviews to a website. It will get noticed. No matter how good you are, website operators are great at sniffing out fake reviews. It's their job to keep their reviews clean and credible. If they didn't police them, no one would trust their sites. So they pay attention.

On a bigger scale, if you post the same review to a bunch of blogs or message boards, people will catch you. You can try to hide it, you can try to vary the message, you can use a bunch of user names. You'll still get busted. It's too easy to search for and compare similar posts. The more you post, the more people know you are posting. As soon as one blogger gets suspicious, they'll look you up and see that you've been posting all over the place.

Guess what happens? All of that positive word of mouth that you were hoping to create turns negative. The very same audience that you were hoping to reach with your fake posts will feel deceived and lied to. And they will start spreading attacks on your company all over the web. You'll lose far more business than you ever could have hoped to gain.

Just Be Yourself

As a marketer, you can comment online, you can post on message boards, and you can do it a lot. Participation is welcome in the new world of online communications and communities. But you have to do it the right way.

The difference between deception and honest participation is *disclosure*.

You can be an eager participant as long as you do it in your own name, clearly identifying who you are and what you stand for. Also, insist that any relationship between your business and the people who speak for you be clearly disclosed from the beginning, whether they are employees, customers, or volunteers.

Sony was busted a few years ago for sending out actors to pose as tourists, asking people to take pictures of them with a fancy new camera. When consumers found out that the supposed tourists were hired by the company, they got angry. They had been used.

Now, let's show how it should have been done. What if Sony had created an exclusive "Sony VIP Tester" program? Let people who are true camera junkies sign up. Sent them loaner versions of new cameras. Given them a membership card, a hat, and a camera bag. Made them feel very, very important.

I guarantee that these people would have talked to far more people than the actors ever could. And they would have done it with a genuine passion and enthusiasm that no actor could ever fake. These volunteers would have been more credible because they had status. They would have felt like important people selected by Sony because they are so special. They would have been proud of their affiliation and happy to disclose it.

Disclosure is a positive thing when done well. Smart marketers understand that disclosure makes messages more powerful because it makes them more trustworthy. Disclosure gives status to participants in a word of mouth program, giving them credibility.

Disclosure is good. Demand disclosure.

Word of mouth is about genuine communications. Always be honest. It's the right thing to do—and it works better.

Staying Honest Is Easy

It really comes down to one simple idea—the *Honesty ROI*. Follow these rules and you'll stay away from trouble:

Honesty of Relationship:
You say who you're representing.

Honesty of Opinion:
You only say what you really believe.

Honesty of Identity:
You never lie about who you are.

Be sure to check each word of mouth initiative you start against these simple rules. It's also important to share these rules with the fans, employees, and agencies who are spreading the word for you. Teach them these rules, and insist that they share the rules in turn with the people with whom they are talking.

Make sure that your company has an internal review process and that someone is asking the tough questions. Many great brands have been deeply embarrassed when an uninformed marketer hired an iffy agency to do a dirty stealth campaign. Make your values clear.

Just Say No

Sooner or later, you'll be offered an opportunity to do something deceptive under the guise of word of mouth. A marketing firm will suggest some secret postings. A junior staffer will offer to go online and generate some buzz.

Don't do it.

If you do even a little stealth marketing, word will get around. And if consumers catch you doing something just a little sleazy, they are going to assume that you're completely sleazy.

This perception snowballs out of control very quickly. In the early days of the internet, pretty much everyone sent email to people who didn't want it. By the time we figured out how much people hated it, the use of all marketing email was tainted.

There isn't a business out there that didn't contribute a little bit to the spam problem.

What happened? Reporters and consumers started referring to all email from businesses as spam, lumping in responsible messages from respected brands with the worst kinds of trash. Everyone stopped talking about honest ways to use email. Few companies fought for anti-spam laws. And the spammers ran free, unopposed.

We must not repeat the unhappy history of email marketing. Your inbox (and your kid's inbox) will never be free of spam, and while email marketing still works, it will always have a reputation problem. We must make sure no one confuses word of mouth marketing, which is by its nature about consumer trust, with the worst kind of deception. If that perception sticks, all of your customers will think you're a liar, too.

Draw a line that your company won't cross. Educate your team. When you see a stealth campaign from someone else, step up and say something. Blog it, call a reporter—whatever it takes. Stealth thrives on secrecy, so uncover it.

You have to step up now to make sure that your reputation and honest marketing tactics don't get tarred with the actions of a sleazy few.

The Rules of Honest Word of Mouth Marketing

1. **Word of mouth isn't stealth.** It's open, honest communications with customers and the community.

2. **Fake word of mouth doesn't work.** You will get busted. When you get busted, the backlash will destroy your reputation.

3. **Oppose all deception.** Protect the trust in genuine word of mouth—for yourself as a marketer and for your family as consumers.

4. **Follow the Honesty ROI.**

Word of Mouth Ethics Checklist

When you're planning a word of mouth campaign, ask yourself the following questions. If you get even the slightest feeling that something isn't 100 percent ethical about a campaign—don't do it! There is no gray area with ethics. (These best practices were adapted from guides we published when I was running the Word of Mouth Marketing Association.)

- ☐ **No Stealth:** We forbid all forms of shill, stealth, and undercover marketing.

- ☐ **No Deception:** We forbid the use of deceptive practices intended to mislead the public about the source of a marketing message or to disguise marketing as consumer opinion or editorial.

- ☐ **True Identity:** Everyone working on our behalf uses their true identity or a clearly identifiable corporate identity. We forbid blurring or obscuring of identity in any way.

- ☐ **Full Disclosure:** We insist that our advocates, employees, and affiliates always disclose their relationship with us, including all forms of compensation, incentives, or samples.

- ☐ **Authenticity:** We insist that all consumers and advocates are free to express their honest and authentic opinion, including negative feedback, without manipulation or falsification.

- ☐ **True Reviews:** We do not request or accept untrue positive reviews or reviews by people who have not used the product.

- ☐ **Honesty:** All information provided to advocates is accurate and honest. We insist that our advocates are truthful with their followers.

- ☐ **No Paid Word of Mouth:** We do not use any form of cash compensation for social media or word of mouth exposure.

- ☐ **No Spam:** We will not insert our marketing messages without permission through off-topic comments, seeding, spamming, bulk posting, or other invasive techniques.

- ☐ **No Cheating:** We never act contrary to the specific rules, terms and conditions, or community guidelines set by each website or venue.

- ☐ **Legal:** We comply with all laws and regulations related to disclosure, advertising, social media, and word of mouth marketing. We do not engage in any practices that violate the letter or spirit of the FTC regulations on disclosure, the WOMMA Ethics Code, or SocialMedia.org's Disclosure Best Practices.

- ☐ **Follow-up:** We monitor word of mouth generated by our campaigns and proactively attempt to correct misstatements, deception, or missing disclosures.

- ☐ **Training:** We actively instruct our advocates and employees on these ethical practices. We require our vendors and subcontractors to meet or exceed these standards.

Just to be sure, ask yourself: Would I be uncomfortable if my family or friends were involved in this campaign? Is there anything about this campaign that I would be embarrassed to discuss publicly?

Word of Mouth Has Always Been Your Best Marketing (You Just Didn't Know It)

Word of mouth has had a far greater impact on your business than you think.

Unfortunately, most businesses do a bad job of measuring it, so they don't always recognize it when they see it. In fact, most marketing reports bury it altogether. The impact of word of mouth is what I call the "hidden statistic."

Problem #1: We Never Call It by Its Real Name

We've just started using the term *word of mouth* in formal marketing. That means that lots of things that should be considered word of mouth are not properly identified as such. This inconsistent naming means that we fail to measure word of mouth accurately.

Take another look at how you describe your sources of new customers. Rename anything that could be considered customer to customer. Give word of mouth its due credit to understand the real impact that it's been having on your business.

Here are some of the customer sources that are actually word of mouth:

- From a friend
- From a coworker
- From my boss
- From my doctor
- Online review or article (not an ad that you ran)
- Direct mail sent to someone else at my company
- Cross-reference on Amazon
- Knowing someone who uses it
- Other
- None of the above
  … and many more.

You probably have a survey, chart, or spreadsheet that reports where your new customers are coming from. It might look something like this:

Now, let's rename those sources of customers that are actually from word of mouth:

When you reveal those word of mouth sources and name them correctly, it turns out that word of mouth is the most important category.

Problem #2: It's Hard to Divide by Zero

You've probably got another spreadsheet that lays out all of your marketing costs and how much business you got from each of them. It might look something like this:

Source	Cost	New Customers	New Revenue	ROI
Advertising	10,000	12	12,000	120%
Direct Mail	7,000	8	8,000	114%
Promotion	9,000	7	7,000	78%
Sales	15,000	9	9,000	60%

What's missing? Word of mouth!

Why? Because word of mouth usually doesn't cost anything. If we don't have a budget for it and we don't have staff assigned to it, we usually forget to add it to our reports about sources of new customers. On top of that, it screws up our spreadsheets, because you can't write a formula to figure the return on a zero-cost word of mouth campaign. So most of us skip it.

Add it in. Take another look, and you'll see something surprising: You're probably getting far more customers for free through word of mouth than from all those other types of marketing.

Remember this: The best value from your marketing investment is the customers you've acquired for free.

The Orphans of Marketing

You've always been doing word of mouth marketing; you just didn't call it that.

Word of mouth marketing is an umbrella term for dozens of different techniques that can be used to energize customers and get them talking. Many of these tactics aren't new, and some are very familiar.

Take another look at some of the specialized marketing tactics that you already know: special sales, loyalty programs, wacky promotions, viral emails, sponsoring a softball team, newsletters, free samples, grassroots political outreach, blogs, partnering with community groups, referral programs, and much more.

These techniques have been used for years by event promoters, small businesses, online marketers, political consultants, loyalty experts, and so on. Now we understand that word of mouth is the thing that ties them all together.

Ask yourself this: "Which marketing programs get people talking about me?"

Most of these programs don't fit into a traditional marketing category such as advertising or direct mail (and you'd have a hard time hiring a traditional agency to do them for you). So they often get neglected or stuck in another department. They are the orphans of marketing.

Many of these orphan techniques actually share a common objective—starting conversations. When we look at them in light of this objective, we realize that what we now call word of mouth marketing is a unified, planable marketing practice.

So let's define word of mouth marketing as a top-level marketing discipline (like advertising, sales, and PR) and place all of the individual techniques you can use within that discipline. Proactively looking at these tactics within the context of word of mouth marketing clarifies the objective and helps you do a better job.

Not only should word of mouth marketing take its place next to other mainstream marketing techniques, it should come first, because it's the cheapest, most effective, and most customer friendly.

Now You Know Just How Important Word of Mouth Is to Your Business

Rescue that orphan.

Put word of mouth at the top of your to-do list. Don't let it get lost, and don't let it get buried under much more familiar traditional advertising programs.

Word of mouth marketing has always been your most important source of new business. It's always been your least expensive source of new customers.

It's time for your most effective marketing strategy to become official, to move out of the marketing orphanage. It's time to create a space for word of mouth marketing in your budget and business plan, set clear objectives, and measure the results.

DEEP STUFF: SIX BIG IDEAS

1. Consumers Are in Control— Get Used to It

Now you know: People are already talking about you, and they're doing it right now. Will you get involved in what they're saying, or will you let their conversations happen without you?

From here on out, no advertising decision will be made again without a new person at the table: the consumer. No longer do ad agencies, media executives, and reporters control the message. Real consumers with real communication power have added their voices to the mix. And their voices are drowning out traditional media. A single consumer voice, in the end, has far more impact than any ad could.

Here's a doozy: Nothing is more powerful than a kid with a blog.

Look at how Google sees it. A customer is looking for information about you. There is only one *New York Times*, and Google only shows a single link to that great article about you that ran last year. But Google will deliver dozens of blog posts about you, right on top, written by just about anyone. Search engines like blogs, and there are far more blogs than newspapers.

Lots of little consumer-written comments, unedited, get far more exposure than any traditional media mention ever will. Word of mouth drowns out advertising and journalism.

This shift in power from media to consumer can be traced back to a few transformative new realities: mass consumer participation, widespread dissemination of consumer opinion, and the scrambling of old-school media with word of mouth.

The bottom line: Word of mouth is now mass media. Here's how it happened.

Mass Participation: We Are Reviewing Like Crazy

From the first time Amazon asked you to write a review, from the first time eBay let you rate a seller, we became a community of armchair critics.

Sharing our opinions has graduated from something small, between friends, to an inextricable part of our culture. Sure, there's always been word of mouth, but it's grown into an active part of our daily lifestyle.

In fact, millions of people write product reviews online. Every major city has websites that let you review contractors, restaurants, stores, and more. Millions more people are writing their own blogs, joining social networks, and reading other people's opinions.

Since Amazon began posting customer reviews on its website in the fall of 1995, more than half of the top online retailers, as well as countless specialized product review sites devoted to sharing consumer opinion, have followed suit. They provide a huge, wide-ranging, and permanent record on the word of mouth about almost every product and service imaginable.

But even more is happening offline, and it always has. Each and every one of us talks to a friend or family member before we buy something. We ask our friends before we bother going to a store.

And we all share what we think about your business, whether or not anyone asked or cares to listen.

People Like Me

It's more than just the fact that everyone is reviewing everything these days.

We don't rely on the opinions of professional reviewers like we used to. We don't just buy *Consumer Reports* and take its recommendations for what stove to buy. We don't blindly follow the official movie reviews. Instead, we listen to our friends—the millions of them who post reviews, have their own sites, and constantly tell us what they like and what they can't stand.

Survey after survey finds consumers using the same phrase—"people like me"—when asked whom they turn to for advice on what to buy. We trust the opinions of people like ourselves more than anyone else. It makes you wonder why companies still pay actors to star in ads, when we'd rather hear from real people.

That trust in real people is being fed by many of the review sites. Amazon highlights reviewers who are willing to post their real names next to their reviews. Many sites let people rate the reviewers, giving you the word of mouth on the word of mouth.

It'd be impossible to meet each one of the people out there posting reviews, but their collective voice—our collective voice—is being heard and followed.

Online stores help this along by giving us the collective opinions of lots of people like us. We don't know everyone who posts online reviews, but we can trust the opinion of a large group. It's hard not to notice 139 negative reviews, in the same way that 400 positive ones mean that something is probably pretty good. Even if you give the opinion of one expert more weight than any one amateur, you can't dismiss an avalanche of criticism or praise.

And if that weren't enough, almost all of the sites that post customer reviews analyze and summarize the data for us. We know the average number of stars a product gets before we even reach the product description page.

No marketer can ignore the fact that "people like me" are out there, and they are sharing what they feel.

Mass Dissemination: What We Say Goes Everywhere

We all remember the classic shampoo commercial. Say it with me: "She told two friends, and they told two friends, and so on." Of course, it didn't really work like that. You told two friends, one of them told her sister, and that was about it.

It all changed when we went online, where mass dissemination is guaranteed. When even a simple email can be picked up by a friend and forwarded to a list of 500 people (who then could forward it to everyone they know, too), word is spreading faster than we could ever hope to control.

Advertisers used to be able to reach 80 percent of buyers with ads on the big three television networks. Now, any old Joe can reach most of your future customers with a few well-placed online reviews. That's a slight change in the balance of power, to say the least.

It's a marketer's fantasy: Could you have a salesperson standing in the aisle next to every one of your products in every Walmart store in the world, saying nice things? Of course not. But regular consumers can say those things on the Walmart website, right there next to the "Add to Cart" button.

Blogs just spread the word of mouth faster. Anyone can set up a free blog in five minutes. They can type what they want about your business, and it's online for everyone to see. Now just because something is blogged, that doesn't mean anyone is reading it. But one blogger links to it, and she tells two bloggers, and they tell two bloggers … you get the idea. Plus, every time a potential customer is researching a purchase, that silly little blog post shows up. It may not be a well-read page, but it's seen when it matters—when someone is ready to buy.

Traditional Media and Word of Mouth Are Forever Intertwined

The professionals used to produce our media for us, but we've lost that clean page of text, written by reporters, edited by editors, and sold in a neat, finished package. We've lost the captive audience watching the pretty ads, displayed on purchased media.

News is now served up à la carte by search engines and bloggers. You don't always see the story as it was originally delivered; instead, you get a link to the middle. You get a random person and her blog connecting what you were looking for to three things you never knew about and then linking to a bigger blogger. The web now inserts rough, raw consumer contributions into web pages, and the search engines grab our messages and combine them with an unruly mishmash of homemade thought. And now the bloggers are the mash-up experts, taking all these messages, rearranging, recombining, and rebroadcasting them to massive, willing audiences.

> **Those who learn how to work with consumers, how to join the conversation, and how to make this work in a positive way will thrive.**

Even a proper newspaper article isn't safe from the consumer voice. Many newspaper websites now link their stories directly to live blog headlines and accept comments from readers, breaking down the clean newsroom wall forever. While the official news story sits static on the page, the links next to it are displayed automatically from anyone blogging or commenting—without an editor filtering the information.

Picture a hard-working young PR rep who lands a dream story about his client in a high-profile newspaper. He emails his coworkers about it and heads off to the boss's office to share the news. But by the time he gets there and his boss pulls up the web page, the story is already corrupted—the blog headlines and comments sitting next to it are horrible.

Your job: Make sure the word of mouth is good. You can't control the consumer conversation, so remember that PR isn't over when the article is written. The goal is to earn good word of mouth on an ongoing basis.

For companies that don't keep their promises, search engines can be even scarier. Let's say that you are spending some big bucks on a search engine marketing campaign. You have nice little ads down the side of the page, all saying, "Click me, we're great." Of course, the bigger links in the middle of the page are from real people. You'd better make them happy, or those posts will overpower any paid placement.

> **When all marketers learn to respect consumers' word of mouth, all marketing will be more honest.**

Let's look at a certain major cable company we won't name that infuriates its customers again and again with missed service appointments, absurdly poor customer service, and other insulting treatment. When you look this company up online, what do you see? Expensive ads, official news stories—and tens of thousands of posts from angry people. It's good to know that the company can never buy another online ad without having it placed next to the words of a customer they've messed with.

Why is this? How can a single blogger with her list of gripes and raves have more impact than *Time* or *The New York Times*? It's because that person is part of a community—a community that seeks out information about things its members care about and shares those opinions through word of mouth. When one of the members of this community rants against some software that accidentally erased his hard drive, that rant gets picked up by a hundred other sites, each with its own following. Anyone tapped into one of these conversations now has immediate access to the rant—and knows which software company killed someone's computer.

There are a thousand websites for every one traditional newspaper or magazine. There are now more independent, individual voices than all of the professional journalists out there. And because these new voices are easier, quicker, and cheaper to access, they travel farther.

Learn to work in this mixed-up world. Know that people are already talking about you in a conversation that is intense, active, and everywhere.

Marketers who ignore the conversation will be seen as aloof and clueless, and they will get kicked around. Those who learn how to work with consumers, how to join the conversation, and how to make this work in a positive way will thrive.

Don't hesitate. Get out there and start talking.

2. Marketing Is What You Do, NOT What You Say

Hey, advertisers! You don't get to tell us what to think about you anymore.

You are not what your ads say or what your brand statement is. You are not what you wish your company to be. You are not the rosy image carefully crafted and projected through a marketing message.

You are the sum total of what people do and feel when interacting with your stuff. You are what real people experience with your company. Write this down:

> You are the user experience.
> UR the UE.

Marketing is what you do, not what you say. The story that will be told by the power of word of mouth is what really happens underneath all the marketing. If you have good products and good services, people will say good things about you. If you fall down on the job, they will say that, too.

With the speed and power of online-assisted word of mouth, you can never hide from this reality. Even a few years ago, you could put out an average product, back it with extraordinary ads, and hope that the feedback wouldn't be heard until enough people had already bought into it. You could put out a bad product and sell it for a long time before people started to realize that it just wasn't any good.

In this new world, you will have product reviews, blog posts, and emails between friends flying around within moments of a new product first hitting the street. You can't push weak products on people when everyone will know within 24 hours whether they're good or not. Great advertising doesn't fix a car that constantly needs service.

When you are thinking about marketing a new product, what you really should be thinking about is what people will say after they use it—about its functionality, its quality, and how you treated them.

Remember the power of the single reviewer? She won't stand for a shoddy product, and she's certainly not going to stay quiet when that product is backed by flashy ads and false promises. Before you can say "primetime commercial," the blogs and reviews will be full of complaints about the real deal.

People who hear about a bad shopping experience are less likely than the people who actually had the bad experience to ever set foot in that store. And when you realize that someone who's had an unpleasant encounter with your stuff is going to tell a lot of other people, you start to see just how damaging bad word of mouth can be in the real world.

Your only choice is to make sure that the experiences people have with your company are positive ones. Make good products. Treat people well. Earn their positive recommendation. Take some of that advertising budget and put it into customer service, because customers' experiences will drive more word of mouth sales than another ad.

You can't fake love—or positive word of mouth. The word of mouth will be about the real user experience of real customers. No amount of advertising will change that.

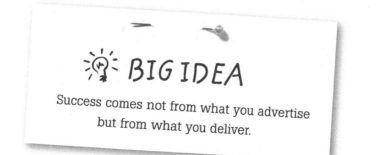

🔆 BIG IDEA

Success comes not from what you advertise but from what you deliver.

Your customers will keep talking about you if your story matches their experience—good service, no hassles, upheld promises. They'll come back to you because you're you.

The sum of your company isn't what you say your brand is but instead the day-to-day qualities that your products and people express to consumers. What really happens underneath all the marketing is the story that consumer-driven media will tell. No amount of manipulation, obfuscation, inundation, or sheer quantity of advertising will save a bad product or bad company.

If you do what you say, if you choose to be a better business, you will do bigger business.

3. The Permanent Record

We used to think that the web was a temporary thing. Now we know the truth: Everything lives forever on Google.

The failed ad campaign, the upset customer, the broken product, the post on a message board, the service rep having a bad day—they will never go away.

So you've got a new job to do. Your mission: Make sure that the good stuff gets on the permanent record, too—the wonderful product, the staffer who went the extra mile, the problem solved, the complaint answered.

Your real job as a word of mouth marketer is to make sure that the human face of your company gets out there. Participate, rectify, engage, entertain, satisfy, support, and surprise.

Correcting the Permanent Record

Let's face it, we all have stuff we'd prefer to let go. It's not that you'll never make a mistake or draw criticism; it's how you handle it that counts. You'll never be able to control the blogosphere conversation. Don't even try.

But what you can do is participate, earn respect, and tell your story. Get started, join the conversation, and be a part of it. You can make sure that the conversation ends on a positive note, that your views are heard, and that you're part of the community.

Start thinking about what kind of experiences you are creating for customers and how those experiences are reflected in the record. Evaluate how customer service is handled and how a botched call will ripple through the word of mouth discussion. And compare that to how a little something special will be remembered and talked about.

A Better Use of $8 per Hour

Here's a tip: Why not recruit one of your customer service reps (preferably one who can spell) to be a word of mouth service rep? Give a low-level frontline staffer the job of proactively searching the web for any and all word of mouth about your company and your products.

When people are praising your company—thank them. When people have a complaint, a rant, a slam—apologize and fix it.

Every problem festering unsolved is another unhappy customer out there spreading negative word of mouth. Make it right. Every problem is an opportunity to fix the permanent record, to end your story on a positive note.

Everyone makes mistakes. Your mistakes live on forever on the internet.

So do the fantastic things you do. Focus on the fantastic.

4. Honesty Is the Essence of Word of Mouth

The one truth about word of mouth is that the truth always rises to the surface. The truth about your company, products, services, and people—your stuff—is all that matters now.

You can't hide a bad product behind a great media campaign. You can't hide bad service behind a big brand. You can't lie to yourself, and you can't lie to your customers.

Word of mouth and the newly empowered customer voice mean that marketers that sell poor products or don't respect their customers can't get away with it anymore.

Word of Mouth Makes All Marketing More Honest

Word of mouth is the feedback loop that forces marketers to pay attention to the consumer. It brings advertisers out of isolation and forces them to confront the reality of the impact that their products and marketing have on real people. It puts the consumer at the head of the boardroom table.

Word of mouth marketing protects consumers by giving them a voice. This kind of marketing gives them a powerful platform—and makes marketers listen. It gives people the power to voice their dissatisfaction and expose dishonesty.

Word of mouth marketers are the ones who have learned to listen. We don't have a choice. We can't do what we do unless consumers are happily willing to relay our message. So we're getting good at making them happy. Word of mouth is on the rise because marketers have finally begun to understand that a happy customer is the greatest advertisement.

Traditional advertising is hurting because consumers don't trust it, they see through it, and they tune it out. When consumers trust marketers, they will recommend their products. When all marketers learn to respect consumers' word of mouth, all marketing will be more honest.

This is a good thing for the future of marketing. All marketers should be held to this higher standard, not only because it's right, but because honest marketing works better.

5. The Math of
Customer Satisfaction

The power of word of mouth fundamentally changes the math of business.

When you factor in the impact of word of mouth, things that look profitable may not be. Ideas that seem smart are often dumb. Unfortunately, not many companies see this because traditional financial reporting doesn't account for word of mouth effects.

Once you understand the math, you'll find that it pays well to treat people well.

One of the big Las Vegas hotels charges $27 per day to use the gym. Hotels are expensive, but that's just insulting. When families get home, what do you think they are telling their friends? "They have a 20,000-gallon fish tank in the lobby"? Probably not. They are saying, "It was nice, but they'll squeeze you for every penny once you get there." This hotel also charges $20 to rent an inner tube at the pool. Good word of mouth isn't spread by parents frustrated because their crying kids didn't understand why Daddy didn't want to get ripped off.

Of course, hotels have done the same thing for years by charging ridiculous amounts for phone calls from the rooms. What's different now is that all hotels are reviewed online. The reviews go up instantaneously, and they never go away. What's different now is that we can talk about these annoying practices with thousands of other people like us. This is exactly the kind of negative word of mouth generator that may make more money in the short term, but hurts your business in the end.

Somewhere there's an accountant with a spreadsheet saying, "Hmmm. Three hundred people a day, 27 bucks a head. That's $8,100 every day, almost $3 million a year in pure profit." The problem is that no one seems to be looking at the other side of the spreadsheet, the side that shows how many customers feel burned by the hotel every day. Traditional cost accounting doesn't report how many betrayed customers decided never to come back to that hotel or how many friends heard their stories. I'll bet they've lost far more in loyalty and room revenue than they take in at the gym.

One of the most famous word of mouth emails ever is a presentation called "Yours Is a Very Bad Hotel," which was created by two frustrated businessmen who showed up late one night at a Doubletree and found that their guaranteed room had been sold to someone else. They sat in the lobby and created a scathing, hilarious PowerPoint about the experience. Millions of people have been forwarded a copy of it over the past few years. Doubletree apologized later, but the damage was done.

Three Math Problems

These days, all marketers are obsessed with measuring results, so let's do some math (actually, some story problems):

Problem #1.

We just spent $100,000 on search engine advertising. Our ad pops up next to three competitors' ads, alongside the regular search results. But the second and seventh results are from the website of an angry customer with the headline "Your Brand Sucks."

What is the cost to our acquisition campaign? How much money did we waste? How much business did bad word of mouth send straight to our competitors' ads? How many people clicked on the negative stories?

Problem #2.

We spent $5 million to develop and launch a new product. Two grouchy customers post negative reviews on Amazon. More bad reviews follow. In fact, with 125 reviews, the average is 1.5 stars (the lowest rating you can get is 1 star). One of the same grouchy customers posts negative reviews on three other sites. Customers never show up.

How fast will this product die? How much development investment was lost because we didn't prepare for word of mouth? What are the ripple effects on the rest of our products?

The Worst Reviews Ever

ACT! was once the greatest contact-management software ever. I actually was given version 2.0 by my dad in 1988 (yes, '88) and used it right through 2004. Then they sold me an expensive upgrade that was just awful.

Hundreds of people agreed. Just look at a sample of some of the headlines from more than 125 negative reviews on Amazon for ACT! 2005:

Major Step Backwards. Don't waste your money on this product. This product is crap! The worst release I've experienced. Slowest software ever written. Every upgrade ruins my database!!! Punishing Users Daily. Avoid this version. Waste of time. VERY BAD PRODUCT. Don't Do It! ZERO stars. Unusable! Rubbish. Disaster. Stay away!!! ... and 100 more.

Wow. That's cold.

But the creators of ACT! took their customers for granted, released a bad product, and word of mouth killed them.

Problem #3.

We pay for an email campaign to one million opt-in (we hope) email addresses. We get one percent click-throughs and close 10 percent of them, giving us 1,000 new customers. But 10,000 people don't remember opting in. So they get angry and decide never to buy from us again. And they each tell five friends that we spammed them. About 2,000 of those people were current clients who are now mad at us. And they each tell five friends.

How many prospects did we lose forever? Is their potential lifetime value greater than the value of the new accounts we acquired? What is the lost revenue from current customers who left because they think we are spamming? What happens when people start blogging that we spammed them?

A Penny Saved Is a Penny Burned

Let's look at another all-too-common example of bad math: outsourced customer service. (I'm not talking specifically about international outsourcing. Poor telephone service is an equal-opportunity offender that spans race, creed, and nationality.)

Company after company tries to save a buck on low-cost customer service. It doesn't work. When you add in the word of mouth math, you realize that any drop in customer service is a marketing disaster.

It comes down to the concept of "first call resolution"—how many customers were satisfied on their first call. When that number drops even slightly, you've created word of mouth poison.

Think about what happens with every person who gets off the phone with a problem unresolved. They get angry. They tell their friends. The word of mouth starts flying, and it's not pretty. Every day that the problem hangs out there unresolved starts another wave of negative word of mouth.

Now do your math. You saved $5 on a low-end call center rep. But the customer has to call twice, so you're paying twice.

Then add in those people who the angry customer talks to. What will it cost to replace those prospective customers?

Bad service is expensive. Especially when you look at the marketing cost to replace the leads burned through negative word of mouth.

This Is a Bottom-Line Issue

Your reputation has real value. You need to factor it into your balance sheet and business plan. Whether in the fundamental quality of your products, the reliability and courteousness of your service team, or a specific marketing or sales effort, you have to take into account the impact of word of mouth on your bottom line.

6. Word of Mouth Marketing Makes More Money

Here's the page that pays for the book. (Show it to your boss.)

Word of mouth marketing is the most profitable marketing you can do. Nothing, I mean nothing, makes you more money. Add these up:

- *Reduced customer acquisition costs.* Word of mouth customers are free. Every one you get lowers your average cost of new business.

- *Free advertising.* Word of mouth promotion doesn't cost a thing.

- *Better results from traditional advertising.* Word of mouth supports your ads' messages and spreads them around.

- *More productive salespeople.* Every salesperson performs better when positive word of mouth is helping them close more deals.

- *More sales leads.* Free prospects come in every day from personal referrals.

- *Reduced customer service costs.* As you answer more questions as part of the public conversation, fewer people need to call.

- *Stronger brand.* Permanent, public recommendations add up to a healthy, positive reputation.

The net impact: more business, higher return on investment, and lower costs. Word of mouth marketing does more than make money on new sales. It makes all of your sales and marketing more effective.

This leads to another important conclusion: Satisfied customers who will spread word of mouth are the most powerful assets you have. So do the following three things for your customers:

1. Protect them.
2. Treat them with respect.
3. Listen to them.

You will do better marketing and be a better marketer because of it. Learn this and you will survive and thrive.

THE WORD OF MOUTH MARKETING MANIFESTO

1. Ethics come first.
2. Happy customers are your best advertising. Make people happy.
3. Marketing is easy. Earn the respect and recommendation of your customers. They will do your marketing for you, for free.
4. Great service starts great conversations.
5. Marketing is what you do, not what you say.
6. Negative word of mouth is an opportunity. Listen and learn.
7. People are already talking. Your only option is to join the conversation.
8. Be interesting or be invisible.
9. If it's not worth talking about, it's not worth doing.
10. Make the story of your company a good one.
11. It's more fun to work at a company that people want to talk about.
12. Use the power of word of mouth to make businesses treat people better.
13. Honest marketing makes more money.

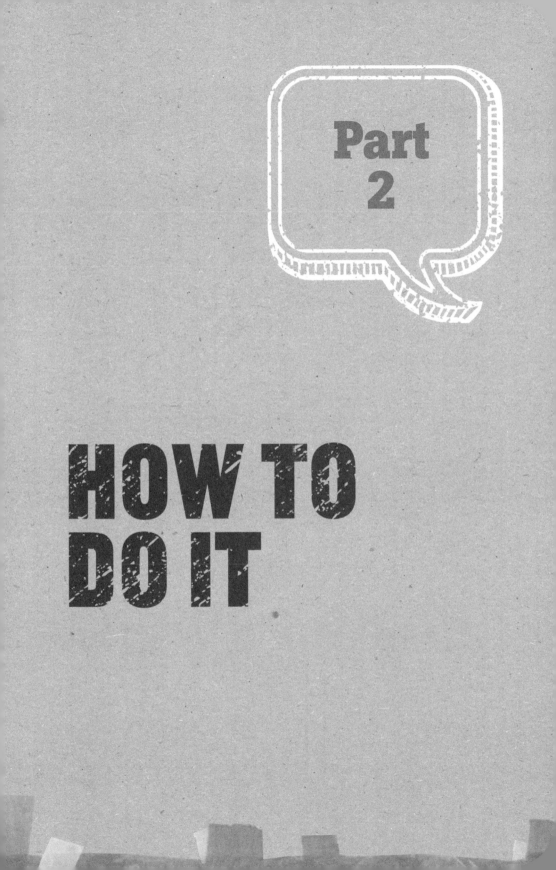

Part
2

HOW TO
DO IT

THE FIVE Ts
IN ACTION

Creating a Practical Word of Mouth Marketing Plan

The first part of this book gave you the background you need to understand the word of mouth phenomenon—why people talk and how businesses should work with word of mouth.

The rest of the book is all about practical steps that you can take to get people talking about you (and help the message spread fast and far). We're going to talk about the hands-on techniques you can use, giving lots of examples that illustrate these techniques in action.

Some of the examples will be things that you can do right away. Some won't apply to your business at all. But everything you read will help give you a feel for the kinds of things you can do to generate word of mouth. When you read the examples and techniques, think about how you would change them to fit your company. There are a dozen ways you could adapt every idea in this book.

Remember, by its nature, each word of mouth moment is original—or no one would be talking about it! Take what you read here as the seeds for ideas, as templates that will help you recognize a word of mouth opportunity when you see it.

So rearrange, rip apart, and rethink everything you read here until it feels like it's right for you. This isn't an instruction manual or a recipe book. There's no specific formula for great word of mouth. Mix and match what you see until you get excited about it. That's when you'll know you've got something that will work.

Finding *Your* Five Ts

To build your plan, you need to walk through the Five Ts and apply each one to your stuff. The following chapters will build out each T in detail. They will explain the most common and most effective techniques and suggest ways that you can use them.

Use the following worksheet as a handy summary and a place to record your plan as it develops. (If you need another copy of the sheet, visit *www.wordofmouthbook.com*.)

The Five Ts of Word of Mouth Marketing

STEPS	WHAT TO DO	EXAMPLES	YOUR PLAN
1. Talkers	Find people who will talk about you	Fans, volunteers, customers, bloggers, influencers	
2. Topics	Give people a reason to talk	Special offer, great service, cool product, silliness, neat ad, new feature	
3. Tools	Help the message spread faster and farther	Tell-a-friend form, viral email, blogs, handouts, samples, coupons, online discussions	
4. Taking Part	Join the conversation	Reply to feedback, participate in social media, join discussions	
5. Tracking	Measure and understand what people are saying	Search blogs, read online discussions, listen to feedback, use advanced measurement tools	

Download this worksheet at *www.wordofmouthbook.com*.

Keep It Easy

People will talk about you if you get the basics right.

A few of the techniques I suggest might be complicated or expensive, but most are easy and cheap. As a rule, start with the simple stuff. It usually works great. Complicated word of mouth campaigns work, too, but they may work only for particular businesses or specific industries. If they won't work for you, that's okay.

Here's an easy one if you've got a website: Put a "tell-a-friend" link on every single page. Make it incredibly easy to spread the word when someone feels the urge. Have that link send a cool email that the recipient will want to pass along again.

> **Each word of mouth moment is original— or no one would be talking about it!**

Here's an easy one if you've got a retail store: Get some great shopping bags, the kind of bags that people will save and use over and over again. Print them with your logo—and some cool, bold design. You'll have a horde of satisfied shoppers walking around, showing you off everywhere they go. People will see the bags, and conversations will start. (Bloomingdale's invented this trick with their "Big Brown Bag." Shoppers like them so much that they actually pay for the bags.) Every shopper becomes a potential word of mouth talker when they have a conversation starter in their hands.

Here's an easy one if you have a restaurant: Give away free food while people are waiting for a table. Every city has a restaurant that does it. Lou Mitchell's in Chicago gives you fresh doughnut holes and Milk Duds. Everybody knows about it, and everybody talks about it. No one is saying, "Hey, you've got to get the turkey sandwich at Lou Mitchell's." But the doughnuts and Duds are the first things anyone mentions when you ask for a restaurant recommendation in that neighborhood.

Whatever business you're in, ask yourself these questions when you're looking at a customer:

- When she walks out the door, what have I given her to talk about?
- How will he remember to tell his friends?
- Could I have made it easier for her to talk to more people about me?
- Was anything about his experience remarkable?

There are hundreds of other ways to get people talking, but you only need one good one to change your business forever. A silly something, a special moment, service with a smile. Anything worth talking about.

Marketing doesn't get any easier than this.

Case Study:
FreshBooks—
A Zillion Little Things

One of the great truths of word of mouth marketing is that you never know which talkers and which topics will kick off a major conversation. Just like traditional advertising. But with word of mouth, you don't need to spend any real money until *after* you know it's working.

You need to try as many little things as you can until you find the ones that people start talking about.

FreshBooks is a service that helps freelancers send invoices. The company wants every designer in the world to try it. When Saul Colt was its "Head of Magic," the FreshBooks team began testing every word of mouth topic they could find:

- Saul saw me writing about a fantastic mustard from Toronto. He mailed me some, even though we had never met. Why? Because he knew I was a talker.

- The FreshBooks team drove an RV between conferences in Miami and Austin instead of flying—and had breakfast, lunch, and dinner with everyone they could. They met 1,500 customers in ten days.

- At another conference, they passed out 1,000 hangover kits, had employees in company shirts acting as volunteer doormen, and held a pancake breakfast in the parking lot. They used their RV to shuttle people from party to party.

- They hired an artist to paint a mural live in a trade show booth. It took three days, and people kept coming back to check on the progress.

- Every time employees travel, they hold a dinner (the "Fresh-Books Supper Club"), where they invite 20 to 30 customers and local bloggers. Customers are shocked when a company calls them and invites them to dinner to say thanks (especially the customers using the free version of the service).

- They have a weekly email newsletter full of contests and love for their talkers.
- Guess what? It adds up. FreshBooks grew from 250,000 to 425,000 customers since starting the nonstop word of mouth campaign.

TALKERS: WHO WILL TELL THEIR FRIENDS ABOUT YOU?

Your Job: Find the People Who Like to Talk About You

All marketing has a medium. An advertisement's medium is TV, newspapers, radio, or any other place that carries ads. Direct mail works through the post office.

The medium of word of mouth marketing is real people.

You need to find the right people to carry your message, just as an advertiser needs to find the right TV programs and publications. Some people will love to talk about you, some won't care, and some may want to talk but have nothing nice to say.

One of the reasons word of mouth marketers place so much emphasis on respect and honesty is because of our reliance on the trust of real people. We must protect the human medium just as carefully as editors protect the journalistic integrity of a newspaper. We owe a deep debt to those who help spread our message, and we repay it by treating them well.

A good word of mouth program is built on finding and taking care of your talkers:

- Identify the right talkers.
- Create a communication channel to reach them regularly.
- Give them the topics to talk about.
- Keep them happy and motivated.

To do these things really well, always remember the three reasons people talk: They love your company, they want to feel good, and they want to belong to a group. Work with these motivations to keep people talking.

Who Are the Talkers?

Usually your talkers are obvious. They are those happy customers who are eager to share their enthusiasm with their friends. Every business has a core of customers who are active recommenders. Sometimes talkers are customers who have the outgoing personality to talk about things they like. Or they may be customers who are less proactive but who are the kind of people who often get asked for advice.

But talkers can be much more than just customers. They can be super-eager fans who will never buy a product. Ferrari has many more talkers than customers. They get word of mouth from noncustomers—eager kids, sports car freaks, reporters, and enthusiasts of all sorts.

When Wynn Las Vegas opened its massive, lavish hotel/casino, it turned to the most important talkers in town: cabbies. The hotel recognized that these are the guys who talk to tourists about where to eat, where to gamble, and where to shop. Before the hotel officially opened, it gave this high-powered group of talkers free rooms and the run of the place. Which hotel do you think the cabbies are talking about now?

Talkers Are People Like Us

There's a myth that word of mouth is only spread by ultra-hip talkers and the cool trendsetters described in Malcolm Gladwell's book *The Tipping Point*. Consultants who sell trend-spotting services have perpetuated this impression. Reporters love to write about the super cool, celebrities, and opinion leaders. But that's not where most word of mouth comes from.

Think of it this way: You know exactly who you'd call right now for help buying a car.

Remember what you've learned—we turn to people like ourselves for word of mouth recommendations. We don't need a paid celebrity endorser (or a celebrity who has been paid off with free merchandise) to tell us what to buy. We want to hear from someone with the same needs and lifestyle that we have. Of course, there are the professionals—the doctors, lawyers, accountants, and electricians—whose advice and recommendations carry the weight of their formal credentials. But most talkers are ordinary, everyday people of all ages, interests, incomes, and status levels.

One active PTA mom recommends more products in a week than any club hopper.

Your talkers are the people who are sending you new customers. Here are some examples:

- Current customers
- The office worker who gets a flyer in the mail and hands it to a colleague
- People who post reviews online
- People in the neighborhood
- A shopper who helps another shopper in the aisle

Discovering the talkers for your stuff is sometimes easy—but sometimes it takes a little ingenuity.

One of the best examples of an organization finding its talkers is The Prostate Net, a nonprofit committed to educating minority men about the risks of prostate cancer and the importance of getting exams. (An awkward conversation, to say the least.)

They created a word of mouth program called the "Barbershop Network." Barbers are perfect talkers. They are opinion leaders in many communities, and they have the time to talk to their clients. The group reached out to 50,000 barbers, taught them how to talk to their clients about the issue, and provided educational resources to pass along.

They put the Five Ts of word of mouth marketing into practice. They identified the talkers (barbers); the topic (the importance of prostate exams); the tool (informational brochures and other educational resources); took part (establishing a dialogue with the barbers); and tracked the results (frequency of prostate exams).

This solid talker program is so much better than what a traditional ad agency would have come up with—probably some cheesy public service announcement.

Talkers Aren't Always Big Spenders

Lots of businesses think that their talkers are the customers who shop most often or spend the most money. That's often not the case. Just because someone is buying doesn't mean that she's also talking.

Your best talker might be your newest customer.

Think about when you talk about restaurants. You probably never tell anyone

Talkers are much more than just customers.

about the place you go every week or the place you stop at for coffee on the way to work. Your favorite joint is so much a part of your everyday life that, like most people, you probably rarely think to mention it to anyone.

But what do you do when you go to a new restaurant for the first time? You tell everyone you see the next day—your friends, family, and coworkers. And a week later, you've probably forgotten all about it.

Your most active, powerful advocates may be the ones who have done business with you only once. They are excited about the experience. They like the product. And they're in a honeymoon period where everything is still great.

You need to think fast—you've got to turn these brand-new customers into talkers on their very first visit. What remarkable experience can you give them to pump up their word of mouth activities?

The lesson: Don't just dig into your customer database and assume that the active customers or big spenders are your talkers. Make sure that you've found the real talkers.

Find Your Talkers

Everything starts with the right talkers.

Each group of talkers will have a different set of interests. Figure out who they are and what pumps them up. Once you know your target talkers, you'll know which topics they like, which tools to use, and how to join in the conversation.

Here are the most common types of talkers. (Use the worksheet that follows this section to help identify your best talkers.)

Talkers #1: Happy Customers

The most familiar talkers are the happy customers you already have.

You know them: those customers who are just so pleased with what you do that they want everyone to do business with you. These are the people who love to tell their friends about you, who mention you first when someone asks about a business like yours. The trick is to learn to separate the customers who are just satisfied from those who are eager to talk.

To find them: Learn to look for signs of extreme interest. Look for customers who come back frequently, who learn the names of the employees, and who are bubbling with enthusiasm.

Be sure your sales team knows that these are important people. It's easy to get annoyed with overeager customers; instead, appreciate that their energy is a major word of mouth asset.

Pay attention to people who fill out comment cards, sign up for newsletters, submit suggestions online, comment on your message boards, or email you. All of these are indications that the person feels a greater connection than a regular shopper. Pay attention to customer surveys and referral programs. A lot of businesses ask, "How did you hear about us?" but rarely do anything with the information. The answer to that question may be the name of your new talker.

Talkers #2: Online Talkers

Look for people who have posted a comment about you on a website somewhere. Look for reviews, raves, and responses.

The fact that someone wrote about you at all is a major step. It shows a special interest in your stuff if someone has the time and personality to post a review. Look for these people because they have the extra motivation that takes them from being a consumer to being a talker.

To find them: Use any major search engine, which will also find mentions in blogs and social media. When you find these talkers, go ahead and make a list. Feel free to email them and introduce yourself, but do not spam them. Remember, when someone writes about a company, they are asking for attention. They'll be thrilled to hear from you.

Talkers #3: Logo Lovers

Anyone who wears your logo is a talker. Hat, shirt, bag, whatever. These are the people who like you so much that they will advertise your brand for free. Do whatever you can to identify and encourage them.

People wear logos for a very simple reason: They want to show that they're part of your group of fans. The need to belong is powerful.

To find them: Make it easy for people to ask for logo items and track who's asking. These are very active talkers.

Logo lovers can't show their support if you don't give them a chance. Give out goodies with your logo. Create an online store with a full line of logo gear. There are sites where you can do this in less than an hour.

Talkers #4: Eager Employees

Your employees can be your most effective talkers.

Assuming you're a good company, many people on your team will have a pride in what they do that is easily transmitted to potential new customers. Not every employee wants to be a talker, but you can identify those with that special team spirit that makes them ideal word of mouth spreaders.

To find them: First, look around. The right employee talkers will be fairly self-evident. They will be the ones with bumper stickers on their cars and briefcases with your logo. We had a new employee who was so excited about joining the company that he sent our electronic brochure to everyone in his online network on his first day of work.

Talkers #5: Listeners

People who listen are often the people who talk the most.

Look for the people who are eager to get information about your company. Someone who cares enough to subscribe to your newsletter or read your blog is hungry to know the latest news. A lot of them will be talkers who want great info nuggets that they can pass along.

To find them: Pay attention to your subscriber lists. Use an email delivery company that lets you track who forwards your newsletters—those are active talkers.

Talkers #6: Fans and Hobbyists

The most hyperactive talkers are often die-hard fans and hobbyists.

Chanel and Gucci didn't build their brands on just the ultra-rich who wear their products. They did it with word of mouth from millions of fans who dream about being able to afford to be customers someday. These eager enthusiasts can become active talkers. Many products—cars, computers, music, movies, and luxury goods—have a similar fan base.

Word of mouth also can be a hobby for certain people. A woman named Harriet Klausner likes to write book reviews. She has a background in library science and has worked at several bookstores. She's posted more than 16,000 reviews on Amazon—just for fun. Harriet is a talker.

To find them: Fans are easy to find—they almost always have websites these days.

Talkers #7: Professionals

There is a special class of talkers who do it for a living: reporters, columnists, critics, full-time bloggers, business networkers, and a whole variety of authors and experts.

Dealing with professional talkers is where we cross into what most people consider the job of the public relations department. Amateur talkers (real consumers) are the focus of this book, but many of the techniques that apply to them also impact what the professionals say.

For most of these talkers, objectivity and evenhandedness are paramount. They're expected to know what they're talking about and will take a credibility hit if they pass along bunk. They have a right to be suspicious and skeptical of your claims, and they won't tend to get overly excited about new products.

> If you've done a good job identifying your talkers, then they should be enthusiastic to hear from you.

But their caution also makes their recommendation more desirable. The professionals we trust earn that trust by being honest and smart. And, because of their reach, they can be catalysts for word of mouth. Particularly for brands that are not well known, being talked about in an influential newsletter, mentioned in a well-linked blog, or featured in a magazine review can be the nudge that gets the positive word of mouth rolling.

Oprah Winfrey is probably the most powerful professional talker in the world. Whether it's a casual mention or one of her formal endorsements (like her book club or annual "Favorite Things" episodes), her word of mouth usually equals instant stardom.

How to Recognize Good Talkers

Talkers aren't all the same. Some people talk to a few friends; some talk to everyone on the planet. Some are convincing; some are full of hot air.

Once you've found a group of talkers, you can look further for the signs that some of them will be extra helpful. Great talkers share the following traits:

Passion

They are excited about your stuff, and they are generally excited about life. True talkers are optimistic and enthusiastic and just love to share their energy. We all know this sort of person—the one who just can't help talking about the new, cool thing that she just discovered.

You're looking for people who care about the topic, invest their time in it, and have strong opinions. Think "dedicated hobbyist." A true foodie isn't making unsolicited calls to tell his friends about restaurants, but he cares deeply about where to eat. Ask him, and he'll tell you exactly where to go and why you'll like it.

Credibility

It doesn't much matter if the cashier at a drugstore recommends a painkiller. You'd rather listen to the pharmacist. Each of them probably talks to the same number of people in a day, but the pharmacist has the reputation to back up the recommendation.

This doesn't mean that talkers must have professional credentials; they just need to have some expertise in what they are talking about. You wouldn't ask your friend the pizza fiend about fine dining, but you would trust his advice about where to go for great deep dish (and a good beer). When you're looking for good talkers, look for those who are devoted enough to the topic to impress others. Often, just being a consumer is enough: If you wear fashionable clothes, people will ask you about fashion.

Connections

Talkers have much more impact when they have a wide network of people they talk to. You want to look for talkers who are members of clubs or associations, who volunteer, who are on a team, or who have many online friends. Quantity often counts when it comes to word of mouth.

Look for certain behaviors that indicate that someone has a sharing personality. Look for indications of how involved and communicative they are. Do they post photos online, have an Amazon wish list, volunteer, or write a blog? Are they members of a networking organization? How many friends or followers do they have in their social networks?

Opportunity

People who are participating in some sort of group activity will have much more opportunity to talk than someone sitting at home. Look for people who are in situations where they will have many interactions with other people.

Travelers are a highly connected bunch of talkers, especially business travelers. They obviously are going to see someone (to whom they will talk) and are possibly going to a large meeting or major convention (where they will talk to a lot of people). Cosmetics companies pay to get their soaps and lotions stocked in the rooms of the best hotels. Food companies want airlines to give out their new snacks. They want to get their products into the hands of talkers who are on their way to a talking experience.

New Talkers Worksheet

PRODUCT WE WANT TALKED ABOUT: _____

WHO WE WANT TO REACH: _____

_____

	TALKER A	TALKER B	TALKER C
Who?			
Who are they connected to?			
Do they have reach and influence?			
What is the WOM topic?			
How do we contact them?			

Download this worksheet at *www.wordofmouthbook.com.*

Your Talker Profile

Now that you've got a sense of who is talking about you, narrow it down. Your next steps:

1. Pick a single group of talkers you want to work with.
2. Create a plan to reach them.

You can't deliver a good word of mouth marketing program that tries to be all things to all people. What motivates one group of talkers will be very different from what motivates another.

If you have found multiple sets of good talkers, that's great. Just go through the Five Ts and create a unique program for each group.

Build a Talker Profile

Write a one-page memo that describes your talkers and why they want to talk. This is your Talker Profile. Don't get fancy. You'll use this to keep you focused while you're planning your word of mouth campaign.

Here's what you should ask in the Talker Profile:

- Who are the talkers?
- What are their basic characteristics?
- What are they already talking about?
- To whom are they talking?
- How do you contact them?

Here's an example for a day care center:

Talker Profile for ABC Day Care Center

WHO THEY ARE: Working parents

CHARACTERISTICS: These moms and dads are busy professionals who drop off their kids at our day care center. They are dual-career couples with active work and social lives. They like day care because they can continue their active lives while knowing that their kids are being cared for and educated.

THEY TALK ABOUT: Child care issues, specifically work/life balance issues. They always want to know how to do more with their kids and still have time for activities without their kids. They like day care because of the freedom it gives them, so they are talking it up.

THEY TALK TO: Other parents, usually in their neighborhood or in the workplace, or to family members. They are also the first to give advice to expecting parents. Some of them have blogs or family websites.

HOW TO CONTACT THEM: We see them every day when they drop off their kids, and we can email them directly.

You can see how this simple exercise starts you thinking about how to work with these particular talkers.

Let's continue with this example. Our day care center wants to enroll more children. We know that our talkers are talking to their neighbors and coworkers, many of whom have kids and child care issues. We could create a word of mouth campaign around a simple idea designed to appeal specifically to these talkers—an after-work babysitting program. If parents could leave their kids at day care for an extra few hours and go to dinner, they would be telling everyone at work about it. In contrast, had our talkers been grandparents, we might have chosen an entirely different topic.

Below is a worksheet for you to complete the exercise for yourself.

Talker Profile Form

Who they are:	
Characteristics:	
They talk about:	
They talk to:	
How to contact them:	

Download this worksheet at *www.wordofmouthbook.com*.

Build a Contact Plan

Now that you know who your talkers are, you need a way to talk to them.

Don't let them get away without opening up some channel of communication. If you can't reach them regularly, then you have no way to influence the word of mouth conversation. The ability to talk to the talkers is one of the key concepts that separates word of mouth marketing from conversations that happen without your involvement. When you find a talker, be ready to connect with them.

Step #1: Get Permission and Contact Information.

When someone in a store shows enthusiasm, ask if you can put her on a VIP list. Offer a coupon or some other special if you need to. When someone writes about you online, send an email asking if he'd like to get insider news in the future.

Don't forget to get contact information. It's hard to talk to them if you don't know how to reach them.

Be careful and polite. Remember that everyone is nervous about getting spammed, and most people are suspicious about any business that wants to contact them.

But don't be shy. If you've done a good job of identifying your talkers, then they should be enthusiastic to hear from you. The right people will be eager to get the latest scoop.

Step #2: Create a Contact Vehicle.

Design an email newsletter, community, blog, or paper newsletter just for your talkers. You can't call them up every time you have a new topic to talk about. You need a simple, ongoing message-delivery system that they can tune in to.

Blogs can come in very handy. Many talkers won't want to be on a subscription list, but they will check in with your blog on a regular basis.

It doesn't really matter how you plan to connect with your talkers—just make sure you can.

Feed Your Talkers

Talkers live on a diet of information. Keep them fed to keep them talking. The word of mouth stops when there is nothing to talk about.

Talkers want to know what's going on. They want the latest gossip. They want to know what's happening before anyone else does. Talkers maintain their expertise and status by being well informed and educated about your products.

Create a steady stream of exclusive information for your talkers. It doesn't matter how you deliver this information. Blogs and email newsletters are nice, but get the information out there any way you can. Just be sure that your talkers are the first to see it.

The off-Broadway hit musical *Altar Boyz* emailed a thank-you note to its audience members after each show. The message also had a special coupon for the talkers to share, giving them the chance to look good to their friends. The email linked them to a website full of goodies to talk about. Photos, downloads, fun postings from the audience, newsletters, and all the usual stuff. The more information you give the talkers, the more they will talk.

Here is what talkers want to see:

- *Detailed data.* You'll be surprised at how much of what you think of as mundane is of great interest to your fans. Talkers are hungry for detail. Share technical data and product manuals. Get geeky.

- *Progress reports.* Talk about new products in development, future menu items, or next season's plans. Let them know what you're working on.

- *Company news.* Remember, talkers want to be family members. Fill them in on the personalities and happenings in your office, the new hires, promotions, and anniversaries. Put a human face on your operation.

A Lesson from Charities—Motivating Talkers

Businesses can take a lesson from grassroots organizations. Charities, politicians, and volunteer organizations are great at keeping talkers happy. It's what they do best.

Motivating and managing volunteers is what makes these groups tick, and they have developed a whole science around it. Every good volunteer manager knows the rules for keeping volunteers happy.

- *Always say yes to a volunteer.* You can walk into any political campaign without an appointment and offer to volunteer, and there will always be a project waiting for you. The secret? Campaigns always save some work for volunteers. For example, when they send out a big direct mail campaign, they always leave a stack of envelopes to be stamped and sealed by hand. Have something ready when your talkers are ready.

- *Make them feel important.* Find a way to make them feel like insiders (and let them show it off to their friends). A political candidate shakes as many hands in the office as on the campaign trail. I still get a holiday card every year from the senator for whom I volunteered in 1988. Show that you appreciate the talkers.

- *Make it fun.* Why in the world do we have those walkathons with the rigmarole of getting per-mile pledges? Isn't there an easier way to raise money than selling cookies? It's because these gimmicks are a lot more fun than going door to door with a tin cup. Make talking entertaining and challenging.

- *Throw good parties.*

There's no better example of the power of taking care of your talkers than the revival of the television show Family Guy. The hysterically funny cartoon was pulled by Fox after just two seasons. The following year, Fox launched a word of mouth campaign to promote the show's DVD.

Case Study: Family Guy— A Little Attention Goes a Long Way

It didn't take long to find the talkers. Hundreds of fan sites were devoted to the show—a real labor of love in the days before blogs, when building a website required buying a domain, hosting, and all the other hassles. These webmasters were special, willing to devote real effort to talking up a show they loved.

These talkers were given status and recognition with a club created for them called the Online Team. Team members were given exclusive access to a private website with video clips, audio files, downloadable icons, private emails, and merchandise. They were given a mission—to recruit more team members. They felt very special.

These efforts made them into even more powerful talkers. The exclusive content gave them lots to talk about. All that content also made their websites richer and more interesting. These little fan sites grew into hubs for thousands of new visitors.

The result? What started as a DVD sales effort turned into a word of mouth movement that did something that has rarely happened in the history of television—the canceled show went back into production and new episodes were put on the air.

The campaign website still remains the link between the show and its fans, who continue to receive all sorts of benefits from continually spreading word of mouth.

Say Thank You

One tool is more powerful than all the others (your folks taught you this one): Say thank you.

Get good at making your talkers feel appreciated and recognized. They will talk ten times as often. You can never say thank you enough, and every thanks is a reason for them to talk even more.

All these talkers are advertising for you, for free. They are supporting your business, bringing in customers, and increasing your profits. These people are out there singing your praises and putting their names on the line for you.

They deserve a little thanks—and, conveniently, thanks is all they want in return for their hard work. They feel like part of the family. A pat on the back from the company (or even a simple acknowledgment that you know that they exist) is like receiving praise from a parent. So don't be stingy.

I'm not talking about gifts, compensation, or cash rewards. I'm talking about *recognition* and *gratitude*. The core motivations that get people to spread the word about you are driven by deep-seated emotional desires to connect with you. A little acknowledgment and a thank you are what they need to cement that emotional connection.

Thank Them Personally

Get in the habit of saying thank you. Say it face to face when you see your talkers. Send thank-you notes. I send more than 100 thank-you notes each month, and they work. Snapshots of my notes are actually posted to a few blogs, and I get a surprising number of thanks in return. It says something about society that so few people get a thank you that it's worth writing about on a website.

The salespeople at Allen-Edmonds shoes send a handwritten thank-you note every time I call and order shoes by phone. I even get a note when I buy from their discount outlet store.

It is important to say a special thanks if you can connect a talker to a specific piece of new business. Take the time to do something to acknowledge that you appreciate what that talker did for you. Web hosting company MediaTemple sent me a credit for a month's free service in exchange for referring a customer. I didn't even know that it was coming, and I never signed up for any sort of rewards program. The gift was that much more appreciated. The same thing happened when Angie's List sent a pound of M&Ms to my wife for referring the site to her sister.

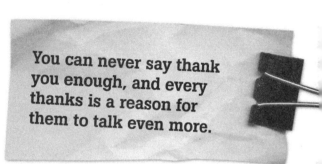

You can never say thank you enough, and every thanks is a reason for them to talk even more.

A great way to thank a bunch of people at once is through special, exclusive benefits. Give them a permanent discount. Send them samples of new products or give them dibs on closeouts. Let them tour the factory. Find creative ways to make your talkers feel appreciated. Talkers who get a cool experience tell everyone about it.

Thank Them Publicly

Recognition is more powerful when it's public.

Think about the awesome power of the high scores list on a video game. A lot of quarters went into Pac-Man machines to get on that list.

Mention your top talkers on your website. Put up a public thank-you page to acknowledge people who have done you a favor. Put your favorite talkers' photos on the wall and their names on a plaque. Frame all the thank-you letters that you get. Give thanks in your newsletters.

On your blog, give prominent links to people who post comments or link back to you. The blog culture is all about mutual recognition, so your thanks will be paid back. On your message board, give the talkers a flashy icon. Find those super-energetic writers and give them special status. Make them look and feel important.

There's a reason why many companies give the best parking space to the salesperson of the month—everyone can see it.

Make Recognition Part of the Program

eBay does a better job than anyone of making recognition part of the fundamental structure of its service. Everyone who has any interaction with the company gets status. Logos, icons, and enhancements show everyone that the active contributors are special.

With a little creativity, you can build similar automatic recognition into your word of mouth program. Create a way to acknowledge talkers wherever they interact with other people. Give them a logo to put on their website.

Membership organizations love to give out membership plaques and lapel pins so their members stand out from the crowd. At conferences, they give out tons of special buttons, ribbons, and rewards to recognize the most important talkers.

Lifeway Christian Resources was selling a new Bible-study course online. It wanted to motivate and recognize its talkers. It created a fantastic tell-a-friend page that let you send an ecard to friends. Senders also entered the country where their friends lived. Each sender was given a web page with a map of the world—with a pin on the map for each country where they sent an ecard. Here's where it gets cool: When recipients sent ecards to *their* friends, the original senders got more pins on *their* maps. Senders could literally see how they were spreading the word around the world. This clever tool gave great recognition to the original senders, gave them a clear sense of the impact of their word of mouth, and was good fun. As you can imagine, many talkers became extremely active, trying to find new ways to get more pins in their maps.

Create a Talker Program

One of the established techniques for connecting with your talkers is to create a formal talker program. This is some sort of official membership group that your company creates to bring talkers together and to give them recognition and status.

A good talker program can be simple. All you need is:

- A web page
- A way to sign up
- Benefits for participation
- A newsletter

If you put these pieces together, you get a home base for your most active talkers that provides both a means of recognition and a communication hub to feed them information.

These programs are often called "evangelist" or "ambassador" programs—but you probably know them by their original name: the fan club.

Fan Clubs

Fan clubs may be the first formal word of mouth marketing programs. Think of 1950s teenyboppers, screaming at the top of their lungs and sending in 50 cents to join the Buddy Holly Fan Club. These days, you see the exact same thing at light speed, powered by instant online communications.

You can have a fan club for anything. Even WD-40.

The official WD-40 Fan Club is amazing. Members get exclusive content, tips and tricks, and lots of fun. They get a weekly newsletter, a membership card, screen savers, and video games they can download. The members even elected an honorary board of directors.

It's all completely fun—and a perfect way to involve, energize, and reward talkers.

Another favorite is the Fiskateers, a fan club sponsored by Fiskars, the scissors manufacturer. You wouldn't think that scissors are that exciting, but when you combine them with the massive craze for scrapbooking, you've got people who care about what they use to cut paper. It's a full-fledged fan club with blogs, message boards, and more. The annual meetings are so exciting that the participants are in tears when they have to go home.

One website, lots of happy talkers.

Ambassador Programs

Maker's Mark bourbon whisky has a very sophisticated ambassador program that takes its relationship with talkers to the next level. In addition to giving its talkers a way of identifying themselves to the company, it encourages its ambassadors to talk about the product and rewards them for being an active part of the community.

When you sign up to be a Maker's Mark Ambassador, you get tons of care and attention. You get your name on an aging barrel of bourbon. You get personal emails from the CEO, invitations to private parties around the country, bar glasses, holiday cards to send to your friends, and (of course) the status that comes from being a member of the family.

Maker's Mark realized that its customers have a greater appreciation for handcrafted bourbon than the typical drinker and that their connoisseurship is something they want to share with others. It has crafted a fun pledge that simultaneously flatters its talkers and asks them to get out and start talking:

> I, as a Maker's Mark Ambassador, do pledge to introduce those who have not yet had the pleasure (poor souls) to the smooth taste of Maker's Mark bourbon. To help friends understand, appreciate and savor what handmade bourbon is all about. To encourage establishments I encounter within my travels to stock Maker's Mark for their thirsty patrons. And to lead by my own example, that every occasion for enjoying bourbon is the perfect occasion for enjoying Maker's Mark.

That pledge pretty much sums up what talkers are all about.

Customer Advisory Boards

For more conservative companies, you can create a customer advisory board. This is a formal program in which customers are invited to give feedback to the company. Sometimes these are small programs with 15 to 20 participants, but you can use the web to open the program up to all of your talkers. Customer advisory boards give you a way to talk to your talkers without explicitly asking them to talk for you.

A program like this has two simple benefits. First, it gets you lots of great customer feedback. Second, it opens up the door for lots of talkers to feel a connection to the company. It gives them a way to participate. And, of course, people who feel appreciated are likely to tell their friends about you.

Rally the Faithful

Customers who are devoted to your stuff love getting together with other people who are just as devoted. People who share the love of a brand are part of an extended family.

So have a family reunion. It turns isolated talkers into a word of mouth army.

The more information you give talkers, the more they will talk.

Harley-Davidson asks on its website: "Who says you can't choose your family?" And they deliver by creating the Harley Owners Group, the gold standard for connecting talkers in the real world. The club has more than a million members in more than 1,000 chapters. Its mission is a simple one: to ride and have fun.

Harley owners take pride in their bikes and look for any excuse to talk about them. Harley gives them that excuse in the form of dozens of statewide and national rallies every year. More than 500,000 people attend the big annual rally in Sturgis, South Dakota. Every gathering supercharges their enthusiasm and gives them something new to talk about.

But you don't need to have the fanatical devotion that Harley-Davidson enjoys to create a space in which your talkers can connect.

Software companies hold developer conferences where programmers get together to talk about technical advances in the software. If these meetings were just about training, the courses could be taught online. But an important purpose is to get talkers together, get them pumped up, and give them a reason to talk about their favorite products.

Getting these people together creates enthusiasm in the community. Let's face it, a lot of programmers lead a solitary existence at work, so bringing 30 firewall administrators together makes them feel like part of a greater whole. If they make a connection to the others in the group (and have some fun), they will want to attend the next meeting, which means that they will stick with the software. And it guarantees that they'll be spreading great word of mouth about the product.

The life of an eBay seller working from home can be lonely, too. So the company brings them all together once a year in an amazing 10,000-person convention/party/reunion/festival called eBay Live! It's a fantastic gathering of ultra-energized people who are thrilled to meet their fellow sellers for the first time. It's a bonding experience.

While the official purpose of the event is to learn skills to be a more effective seller, the real purpose is to generate enthusiasm. Between sessions, attendees wear silly hats, swap collectible pins, and attend the official eBay dance. There was even an eBay community cookbook one year. Those attendees come home giddy with enthusiasm for the brand and become stellar talkers.

Simple Events to Keep People Talking

You don't need a convention to make this work for you. Just think about the easiest way to get your talkers together.

If you have a store, host a cocktail party, live music, or a book reading. It doesn't matter what the reason is; just create an excuse to invite everyone over. For years, I've traveled around the country hosting a series of networking dinners called the "Feast for Smart Marketers." There's not much to it—I book a banquet hall in a Chinese restaurant and invite everyone I know in town. No speaker, no panel discussion. Just 200 people and lots of great food. Pretty much all of my customers and lots of great word of mouth come from these simple dinners.

Case Study:
Microsoft's MVPs—
Energizing Talkers

Microsoft's MVP program is the classic example of reaching out to your talkers and making them feel fantastic. It has been going strong since 1992—long before blogs and social media. It has grown into one of the greatest word of mouth programs in history, and it's so simple that anyone (with any size budget) could do it.

An invitation to the program is now an annual reward that says thank you to 4,500 talkers in 90 countries. Here's the recipe:

1. *Find the talkers.* Microsoft surfs the message boards, blogs, communities, and offline events to find the most engaged and credible talkers. They look for people who love a particular piece of software and are the kind of personalities who love to help other people.

2. *Surprise them.* MVPs get a letter announcing that they have been selected. They also get a keepsake box with the surprise gift of the year, usually something to show off, like a computer bag or a desk set. The gift has become legend, generating tons of anticipation and speculation.

3. *Make them feel special.* Microsoft will send a letter announcing the prestigious award to three people chosen by the MVP. MVPs have these letters sent to their bosses, college admissions officers, and spouses. And the MVPs credit these letters for getting them promotions, into college, and a little more peace at home.

4. *Engage them.* All year the MVPs get private talks with the product developers, an advance look at software, and behind-the-scenes information. They actually get to meet the people who build the software they love. Microsoft hosts more than 500 live web meetings, chats, and webcasts each year just for the MVPs, more than one a day.

5. *Have fun.* The annual MVP Summit in Redmond has become a must-attend pilgrimage for the MVPs. Microsoft pays for everything; participants just have to get there. MVPs love connecting with fellow MVPs and the product developers. Bill Gates or Steve Ballmer shows up, and there are plenty of social events. For those who can't make the big event, there are local meetings all year long.

The big secret: It's about finding a way to tap into existing talkers and existing passion. You could do most of this starting tomorrow.

TOPICS: WHAT WILL THEY TALK ABOUT?

Your Job: Give People Something to Talk About

All word of mouth starts with a topic of conversation. People won't talk about you if you don't give them something to say.

Anything that catches attention is a topic. Anything that catches attention and then gets talked about is a fantastic topic. All sorts of things can be good topics: a fabulous freebie, a moment of great customer service, a special dessert, or an unusual advertisement.

Zappos, an online shoe store, allows no-questions-asked, 365-day returns with free shipping. Yep, you can keep the shoes for a year before returning them. I doubt anyone returns their shoes that late, but it's a fantastic reason to talk.

It's Not Your Mission Statement

A word of mouth topic is not your official marketing message or your formal brand statement. It's a simple message that sparks interest and conversation.

Great word of mouth topics are often hard for traditional marketers to see. They violate the rules of marketing. They aren't planned, they aren't corporate, and they are rarely official. It's an exception when real people want to repeat your official company motto or carefully crafted theme. Instead, people latch onto the *unexpected*.

RedEnvelope is an online gift catalog. They have nice stuff but not necessarily nicer than any other good catalog. Their motto: "RedEnvelope's mission is to make gift giving, no matter what the occasion or circumstance, simple and fun." That's fine, but nobody is going to repeat it.

> **People won't talk about you if you don't give them something to say.**

But they have a killer topic: Every item comes gift wrapped in the most gorgeous, elegant, impressive red box with a giant bow. People who receive gifts from them can't help but talk about the wrapping. (They talk about the wrapping more than the gifts.)

The wrapping is a perfect word of mouth topic. It makes people want to talk, and it's easy to talk about. When most people get a gift from a catalog, they rarely remember the catalog, just the item and who sent it. RedEnvelope's box creates instant word of mouth. When one of these boxes is opened at a party or a baby shower, a whole roomful of people are talking about it.

Every company, every product has at least one great topic. Your job is to find it and give people something to talk about.

Now, to be totally honest, sometimes finding a topic is pure luck. You'll try a lot of things; you'll put out some interesting ideas. No one will talk about what you ask them to, and everyone will start talking about something completely different.

Finding a Great Topic

Don't overthink this. The topic that works best for you will be something so simple, and possibly so silly, that you may miss it. Good word of mouth topics are the kind of great, easy ideas that get buried by bureaucracy in a corporate planning session.

Lower the bar, keep your mind open, and expect that it may be your intern who comes up with the most amazing word of mouth topic.

There are three rules to developing a great topic: keep it simple, organic, and portable.

Good Topics Are Simple

Keep your topic short and sweet. It should be developed around a single idea that's easy to repeat.

A few hotels have begun to figure this out. The Hotel Monaco chain wants to be thought of as cool and fun. So they offer each guest an in-room goldfish. That's something you tell a friend. Westin did years of research to create the Heavenly Bed, a bed so nice that you'll talk about it the next day. (Every other chain has copied them, so they need a new topic.)

Quiznos is giving Subway a run for its money with the idea of hot, toasty subs. Even though Subway always had them, Quiznos made it the topic of conversation.

If you're a cheesehead like me (a Wisconsinite), then you love cheese curds, little lumps of cheddar that are squeaky when they are fresh. During a car trip though central Wisconsin, my wife and I drove past a giant billboard with the words "Squeaky Curds" and an exit number. Must ... get ... curds.

Twenty miles later, we ended up at the Carr Valley Cheese factory in tiny La Valle, Wisconsin. We had some curds. They were amazing, fresh, and oh-so-squeaky.

They also had unbelievable, rare, and ultra-gourmet prizewinning cheeses. The kind that you only find at exclusive cheese shops. We bought a ton. We sent some to a friend who is a New York City chef. We've turned into true talkers.

But when we talk, we talk about their squeaky curds. We've brought a lot of people to the store, and we've sent a lot of mail-order gifts. You can't explain a great half-sheep, half-goat smoked feta as easily as you can say, "You gotta try these curds."

Carr Valley Cheese picked its topic correctly.

A great topic is more simple than you think. Resist the urge to make it complicated.

Good Topics Are Organic

Good organic topics are based on the exceptional qualities that make your stuff stand out. It's about being buzzworthy. These are usually the most sustainable topics around.

BIG IDEA

Word of mouth is as much about product features as it is about marketing.

Design and features are worth talking about. They provide topics that flow naturally from a product's attributes, without much need to be pushed by marketing.

If you want long-term, deep-seated word of mouth that creates a fantastic brand, then you need more than a one-off promotion. You need to work to create products that people fall in love with and are compelled to share with their friends.

Start asking, "Would anyone tell a friend about this?" in every meeting, in every department. If you don't get a resounding "Yes!" then you need to add something.

Good Topics Are Portable

You need a topic that's easy to move along.

Entrepreneurs are always looking for an elevator pitch, which is a story you can tell an investor while in the elevator of a 20-story building. That's way too long for word of mouth.

You need the pass-in-the-hall test. Try to fill in the blanks with your stuff:

- "You should try _____, it's _____."
- "Can you believe _____ did _____?"
- "There's nothing better than _____ for _____."

There should never be an *and* anywhere near your topic. Topics don't work as well when they become lists. ("Try us because we're friendly, affordable, experienced, have great customer service, and give you free ice cream while you wait.") Your topic should be repeatable within a second or so. ("We give you free ice cream while you wait.") Otherwise, no one will remember it.

Amazing Topics Are Unexpected

Listen very carefully to your customers. They are probably already talking about something—and it may not be what you were expecting.

That's okay. Go with it.

Whatever gets your customers excited is a great topic. Don't worry if your marketing plan says to promote speed, but people are talking about price instead. Don't panic if your exciting stain remover turns out to be a great weed killer.

Hidden features and unexpected uses are some of the best word of mouth topics you'll ever get. (Your advertising people will get grouchy and try to squash this organic message for a canned one that they created. Ignore them.) If people are talking about something unexpected, it's not wrong—it's an opportunity.

Did you know that kids are making prom dresses and tuxedos out of duct tape? This is a great word of mouth topic that was totally unexpected.

Duck Tape brand duct tape spotted the fad and encouraged it. They now have an annual "Stuck at Prom" contest to award college scholarships to the most creative couples. Hundreds of couples enter every year, representing thousands of hours of work and an immense amount of word of mouth. Check out the winners at *www.stuckatprom.com* and see how many people you tell.

Taking Care of Your Topics

It's not over after you've found a topic. You need to keep improving it and massaging it to make sure it stays relevant and effective.

Test Your Topic

The only way to know if you've found a good topic is by trying it out in the real world. No amount of planning will help you know in advance. Test it.

- *The telephone game.* Can your topic get passed along from person to person at least three times and come back to you recognizable?

- *The high-school test.* Ask a teenager if you're buzzworthy. A glimmer of interest means that you're on to something good.

- *The customer test.* Leak your topic to a customer or two and watch what happens. Do they respond to it? Do they repeat it? Does anyone new come into the store and ask you about the topic?

Keep It Fresh

Topics do go stale after a while.

Unfortunately, the more people talk about something, the less interesting it is. Success can eat away at a topic's effectiveness, because the motivation for word of mouth is often to share inside information.

I helped promote a new marketing conference primarily using word of mouth. We had great success with a companion blog and podcast that featured interviews with all the speakers before the event. It was original and widely talked about.

So we did it again—and results were disappointing. Everyone already knew about the blog and podcast, so there was no reason to talk about them. We started looking for a new topic.

Don't Drop Your Topic

Here's something to watch out for: Once you have a successful topic that is creating good word of mouth, you have to keep it up. Your commitment to the topic will set you apart just as much as the topic itself. If you ever stop doing whatever you were doing to get attention, people will notice.

A word of mouth topic is not your official marketing message.

How much do you like the Milwaukee airport? Would you stop there even if you didn't have to?

Midwest Airlines had a good thing going with two strong topics and a devoted following because of them. The airline provided first-class-style seating at coach fares. Every person on board was treated like a high-status passenger, enjoying everything from the amazing meals served on china to the cushy, two-across, big leather seats throughout the cabin. Topic number two was pretty cool, too. They baked chocolate chip cookies on board every flight.

And really, who doesn't like being treated like a first-class flyer? Who doesn't like fresh-baked cookies? People loved it, talked about it, and started to opt for an extra stop in Milwaukee (Midwest's hub) just to get on board.

Then Midwest launched its Saver Service, offering clients coach seating and lower fares. No leather, no china, only occasional cookies. Customers who wanted to pay more for all the previously standard bells and whistles could still do so. But, of course, people wanting to pay more for first-class treatment can do that with any airline.

Midwest found a way to cut costs, and they also cut out the topic that was the basis for their stellar word of mouth. No one is talking about them anymore.

Step 1: Find a Topic You Can Use Today

I promised from the beginning that you'd get word of mouth strategies that would get people talking right away. Here they are.

These are simple things you can do to get people talking immediately, without spending a lot of money and without fundamentally changing your business. (Keep reading for some more sophisticated topics that require a bit more effort.)

Special Sales

The easiest topic you could possibly create is a good sale or special offer. You could put down this book, discount a favorite product, throw a sign up in the window, and someone will tell their friends. It doesn't take a lot of finesse to bring people in and get them talking about a sale. Sales are a long-proven word of mouth topic.

Although sales won't keep people talking forever, they create bursts of conversation.

Give it a little extra oomph by coming up with an unusual offer. A buy-one, get-something-not-normally-for-sale offer; something crazy; or a catchy theme. You can get a lot of conversations going with a creative message.

Keep the word of mouth moving with the sure-thing tool of exclusivity, or even just the appearance of exclusivity. These days, it's common to get an email with a "secret" discount coupon supposedly just for friends and family of employees. Of course, these are designed to leak out and spread across the web. So create a special offer, put it in an email, and ask your employees to share it with their friends. Employees will be happy to be talkers, and they get the status of being able to hook up their friends with a deal. Word of mouth will take care of the rest.

Extraordinary Customer Service

"They treat me well" is an awfully powerful word of mouth topic. Nice guys, in this case, finish first.

It's not hard to get noticed when you do something special for your customers, because very few companies bother. With so little remarkable customer service these days, anything generous, respectful, or creative will get talked about.

The great thing about terrific customer service is that it works for every type of business.

The handyman who takes his shoes off every time he enters your house or the delivery people who willingly dispose of your old stuff get extra credit for themselves and generate solid word of mouth for their companies. You're more likely to refer your friends to movers who deliver extra boxes to you, to self-storage places that offer a free loaner truck, or to the real estate agent who sat at your new house and waited for furniture to be delivered.

LensCrafters fixes glasses for free, even if they were bought somewhere else. Headsets.com, a $30 million online store, sends a thank-you email after each order—with the direct phone number and email for the CEO. Sears lets you return or exchange major appliances, no questions asked, within 90 days. That's a big deal if the refrigerator that looked great in the store looks terrible in your kitchen. These little extras earn extra word of mouth.

PrintingForLess.com has become one of the most popular printing companies in America through extraordinary customer service. I once ordered a small batch of brochures. An employee actually went to my website and noticed that the logo on the brochure was a slightly different color than the one on my website. She called to make sure it was okay. Then she fixed it for free. All that service for an order worth less than $500. As you can imagine, they get a ton of word of mouth from my team.

Look at your customer service from a word of mouth perspective. Are you set up to give people a reason to talk? Or a reason to talk negatively? When someone gets off the phone with your company, what will they tell their friends?

Think about those little extra things you can do to make people talk about you.

Do Something Silly

Businesses are way too serious these days.

Make people smile and they will talk about you. Humor may be the best medicine—it's also a super word of mouth topic.

Do you feel an emotional attachment to your backpack? JanSport knows that a lot of people do and offers them a very special lifetime warranty. You don't send your bags in for repairs. You send them to "Backpack Camp" for a little vacation. You even get a cute postcard from your bag, telling you all about the fun it is having at camp and letting you know when it's coming home.

Sometimes the silliest topics arise from product names themselves. Is there anything amusing or memorable about foundation repair? Not unless you're dealing with The Crack Team, a St. Louis-based company that is widely known because of a beloved mascot, Mr. Happy Crack, and a wacky motto: "A dry crack is a happy crack!" Mr. Happy Crack has his own line of apparel and his own website, but he's best known for generating business for The Crack Team. The company has a reputation for great work, but it wouldn't have grown to nationwide acclaim if it weren't for its word-of-mouth-worthy name.

Potbelly Sandwich Works didn't take itself too seriously when one of its Chicago stores was covered with construction scaffolding. Neighboring stores hung the usual cheap banners announcing they were still open. Potbelly took advantage of the opportunity and turned their banner into a word of mouth topic. Their sign: *Look! A Sandwich Joint Disguised as a Construction Site.* How many people walked past that sign, told a coworker, and ordered some lunch?

Silly doesn't have to be complicated. For years, I've been publishing newsletters with names like "Damn, I Wish I'd Thought of That!"

and "You Can Be a Word of Mouth Marketing Supergenius!" These newsletters are good, but the names get them noticed and forwarded.

Partnering with a Charity

Partnering with a charity gives you an immediate topic. People tell their friends, "Buy from that store. It goes to a great cause." It's a genuine chance to do something good and a proven way to start positive word of mouth.

If you're promoting a conference, donate tickets to charity and auction them off. Sometimes you'll get far more publicity and word of mouth from the auction than from the rest of your marketing. Similarly, many of the stores that sell stuff on eBay for you offer to waive their commissions for local churches that want to sell donated used goods to raise money. It doesn't cost the store much—and everyone in the church talks about it.

From a word of mouth perspective, charities are especially powerful because they come with their own built-in network of talkers. When you connect with any nonprofit, from a national organization to a single, small youth group, everyone in that group has a reason to talk about you. They are organized, involved, and have ready-to-go communication channels.

Think about the talkers when you pick a group to partner with. Donating to the Red Cross won't get you a lot of special attention. It's too common. An unusual cause or a local group may be much more excited about the relationship. You're well within the bounds of good taste if you ask the group to send an announcement about your contribution.

Step 2: Create a Campaign Worth Talking About

Your next best topics will come from campaigns that you launch specifically to generate word of mouth. These aren't as quick as the instant ideas above, but they aren't too hard, either. You can probably get most of these going in a few weeks.

Repeatable Advertising

Good advertising can be the topic of a word of mouth campaign. From Wendy's "Where's the Beef?" to Budweiser's "Whassup!" campaign, ads that stick in the mind start up the conversation.

Repeatable ads work because they get word of mouth. Word of mouth works when it's created by a repeatable ad.

We like to talk about advertising. In fact, a substantial amount of what we consider word of mouth about products is actually about the *advertising* for the products. You can't guarantee that an ad will be worth talking about, but it's worth trying.

You should try to build word of mouth into every advertising campaign.

Staples came up with a great ad campaign with a good motto: "That was easy." The ads featured an "Easy Button" that you could press to make life easier. They turned it into a word of mouth campaign—with impact far beyond the advertising—by selling toy Easy Buttons in their stores. They've sold more than a million buttons. People put them on their desks. It gets talked about in a million offices. (They donated the income to charity.)

When you advertise, you are putting out a lot of cash to tell something to a large number of people. Wouldn't it be nice if those people repeated it?

Viral Campaigns

Viral campaigns are email messages specifically created to be forwarded to lots of people. The content can be anything: coupons, newsletters, or product updates. But they are usually some kind of game, joke, or funny video.

This technique is used so often that some people think that viral email is the same thing as word of mouth, but it's just one of many things that you can do.

There is no secret formula here. Hire a designer, create something fun, and send it out. Chances are, in between the few work-related messages you have, your inbox is crowded with forwarded stuff that your friends and coworkers think you will want to see. All that stuff is viral.

There's a lot of luck involved, and sometimes just good timing. You can create a great email, send it out, and it may get passed along instantly to millions of readers. Or it may go nowhere.

> **Long term, sustainable word of mouth comes when a business becomes truly immersed in the word of mouth philosophy.**

Viral emails may be kind of dumb, they may even be completely unrelated to the product, but they do get attention. Not all marketers are fans of this technique. Some think it's a little forced, with little genuine connection to the positive qualities of your brand. But when they work, they spread amazing amounts of word of mouth.

The most reliable viral topic is a simple coupon. A few years ago, my interns started coming into the office all jittery and wired. I thought we had a drug problem.

We did. It was a coupon being sent around by email offering a free coffee at any Starbucks location inside a Barnes & Noble bookstore. There were lines out the door as the email was forwarded back and forth across the city. All the books and fancy lattes they sold were probably worth ten times the cost of the free coffee.

It's important to note that technically you can't create a "viral" anything. Viral is an adjective that describes what happens when something gets forwarded to an enormous number of people. You can create something really interesting, start the word of mouth, and hope it goes viral. Saying you're going to create a viral video is like saying you're recording a Top 40 song. You can only record a great song, promote it, and hope it goes Top 40.

Free Information

Giving away free content is a great way to get people talking.

Give them market research, reports, white papers, webcasts, newsletters, anything. Free information provides rich, meaty topics that are perfect for starting word of mouth conversations. As you put more and more information out there, you feed deeper, more relevant discussions. Your talkers also look and feel smarter when you give them more to say. Someone is much more likely to talk about new research that you have just given them than a one-off promotion.

Best of all, most of these items are portable, easy to share, and cheap to produce.

I created a series of short articles and put them on my website as free downloads. These simple, one-page documents are each less than 500 words. They have been downloaded more than 10,000 times, and most have been passed along by email. Salesforce.com shares the video, audio, and presentations from every conference that it has ever done. It is an incredibly valuable storehouse of content that makes its product that much more useful. It's also a constant conversation starter around the office. Book publishers take advantage of the opportunity to share the first chapter of a debut novel to create buzz and get people reading.

Without a doubt, the most powerful thing you can give away is a free weekly email newsletter. It's easy to produce, relevant to the reader, and easy to pass along. If you don't have an email newsletter, start one today.

Some people worry that giving away too much information might undercut the value of their products. It never happens. The stuff you share proves your expertise and attracts customers. It makes them want to talk *about* you and *to* you.

Wacky Stunts

The Wienermobile: generating word of mouth since 1936.

A high-profile stunt can create an instant topic that gets tons of word of mouth. It won't necessarily create deep, sophisticated con-versations about your brand, but it will get you talked about.

Jones Soda doesn't have the resources to out-advertise Coke and Pepsi, but they know how to generate word of mouth. One Thanks-giving, they created a whole series of nasty, awful soda flavors, including Brussels Sprout with Prosciutto, Broccoli Casserole, and Smoked Salmon Pâté.

Undrinkable. But talkable.

I'm sure we weren't the only family who had a taste-test party. Any-one who saw these flavors is talking about them, and they are sure to notice the normal flavors next time they are at the store.

One of the wackiest stunts I've heard of is the story of Half.com the website and Half.com the town. Half.com was a marketplace web-site much like any other. In the dot-com boom, they needed attention like everyone else. What's a site to do? Well, they convinced a small town in Oregon (population 345) to change its name from Halfway to Half.com for a year. This first-of-its-kind coup landed Half.com on the map (literally) and generated substantial national publicity and gobs of word of mouth.

Yahoo! loves high-profile publicity stunts that get people talking. On their tenth birthday, they partnered with Baskin-Robbins to give a free ice cream cone to anyone who downloaded a coupon. Target showed up in Manhattan on a sweltering day with a truckload of $99 air conditioners. They didn't even have a store there, but everyone was talking about them. And there's the always-buzzworthy Nathan's hot-dog-eating contest.

A great stunt doesn't need to be expensive or complex. Just fun. Hold a contest. Host a party. Hire guys in Elvis suits. I saw an inflatable dinosaur and a robot hand in a store window. Nothing fancy, but kids were coming from all over the shopping mall to check it out, and they brought their parents.

Step 3: Become a Buzzworthy Company

The best topic of all: being a company worth talking about, all the way through.

Long-term, sustainable word of mouth comes when a business becomes truly immersed in the word of mouth philosophy. Your brand becomes fundamentally talkworthy as you reach inside your company and change how you think about business and your relationship with your customers.

These changes aren't easy. Sometimes they're radical. Not every company can make it happen. But your success is locked in if you can create a truly buzzworthy experience. You transform from a business that is constantly pushing out messages through expensive advertising to one that is pulling in customers, for free, through word of mouth.

Great Products

Extraordinary products create sustainable, long-term, company-changing word of mouth.

Create irresistible things, and people are guaranteed to talk forever. Unfortunately, there's no way to teach you *how* to do this. It must come from within.

Viking stoves. Moleskine notebooks. Corky's BBQ. Tiffany diamonds. Manolo Blahnik shoes. See's Candies. Peter Luger's Steak House. The things that make you go *oooh*.

In all of these cases, the topic is clear: People love the stuff.

Uniqueness

"Did you know about _____?" is the start of so many word of mouth conversations. We like to share topics that are surprising, special, and one of a kind.

Be unique. Do things that are, by their nature, an interesting topic of conversation.

Try to create topics that only you can be associated with. This feels a bit like the classic marketing concept of *positioning*—owning a unique place in the customer's mind. In this case, you want to own a unique place in the customer's conversation.

Nike lets you order completely customized shoes, with your own style, color, decoration, and personalization. Anyone who owns these will be talking about them. And everyone who gets talked to will know that the shoes are Nike.

The Trader Joe's grocery chain has built a word of mouth empire on the power of unique products. The entire store is full of unusual house-brand items that are fantastic—and available nowhere else. They sell a bruschetta topping that my parents (who live in Florida) are nuts about. They make us mail it to them from Chicago. My dad tells his friends, who tell their children. The last thing I heard, the daughter of a friend of a friend of my parents was trekking 90 miles to Chicago for a $3 condiment. Multiply this by 300 products that you can't get anywhere else, and you have a sense of how powerful uniqueness can be.

Crayola's R&D geniuses invented Color Wonder magic markers that only work on special paper—and not on walls or children. This is so good, it practically speaks for itself. Every parent who tries them is on the phone immediately, telling every one of his or her friends.

A Shopping Experience

Do you want everyone who visits your store to become an instant talker? Make your entire store a topic. Turn the joint into a word of mouth experience.

People want to do more than shop. That's why the absurdly enormous Mall of America gets 42 million visitors each year.

Adventure outfitter REI lets you test climbing gear on in-store, three-story climbing walls and test shoes on simulated mountain trails. They teach classes on how to use their gadgets and how to master a variety of outdoor activities.

This works for local, small businesses also.

Laura told Julie who told Andy who told Karen about...a dentist. The husband-and-wife team at Delaware Dental, in Chicago, have turned their practice into something special by creating a "dental lounge." The office is decorated in funky, modern colors. Instead of the pan-flute version of the Beatles' greatest hits, they ask about your musical taste on your patient information form. The topic: a unique atmosphere that makes a routine visit remarkable.

Take a look at how a bridal salon would create an experience. It's not just about the bride. Our talkers also are mom, little sister, best friend, and the bridesmaids. Give them an experience. Create a comfy place to hang out. Feed them well. Keep them entertained. The bride's gang will have far more word of mouth conversations than the bride herself.

Build It into Your Brand

Some companies are built from the ground up to work through word of mouth. The topics are obvious, because the reason to talk is the essence of their business plan.

There are a lot of ways to buy insurance on the internet. Progressive Insurance helps its customers by providing the price quotes from its competitors, even when the competitors' prices are better. That's a topic worth talking about. They built an entire company around a word of mouth concept, with no real risk, because buyers are checking prices anyway. The entire concept of the company is woven into the word of mouth topic.

Best Buy's computer repair service is perfect for word of mouth: It's called the Geek Squad. The staff wear nerdy uniforms. They drive special Geekmobiles that are usually parked on the sidewalk in front of the store where everyone can see them. Every bit of the concept makes you want to talk about it, even when you don't need computer repair. And you'll remember them when you do.

You can make a company word-of-mouth-ready by choosing customers who are also talkers. My parents once owned a one-hour photo lab. Their customers were random shoppers off the street and were hard to reach without big advertising. So they sold it and opened a specialty photo lab that catered to professional photographers and advertising agencies. Those are communities of tightly connected talkers who know each other and talk to each other. It worked so well that they didn't even need a storefront with expensive rent—they moved into the fourth floor of a nondescript office building. People knew where they were through word of mouth.

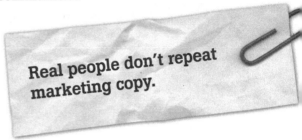

Real people don't repeat marketing copy.

The Demeter Fragrance Library isn't your regular collection of perfumes. If you really want to, they have perfumes that will make you smell like rye bread, tomato, or Play-Doh. Would anyone want to spray on a little lobster or earthworm? The word of mouth from the unusual scents got them the breakthrough they needed in a tough business—enough to get them stocked at major cosmetics counters.

You don't see many brands that are built for word of mouth. It's hard to do. It takes a top-to-bottom commitment to make it happen. But it's something to strive for.

Case Study: IKEA— Tons of Topics

You never forget your first trip to IKEA. Mine was in college. My roommate James initiated me into the cult. We drove 30 miles for some cheap furniture and a chance to see what all the talk was about. In the past 20 years, I have initiated dozens more people and probably brought IKEA tens of thousands of dollars in word of mouth sales.

A visit to IKEA is a fun day trip instead of the usual furniture-shopping hell. It's almost like going to Disneyland.

Here are five word of mouth topics built into a single shopping experience:

- *Surprising.* You always find some crazy, fun items that you never expected. Like a $15 turtle-shaped chair.

- *Kid friendly.* Shopping for furniture with toddlers is usually a recipe for disaster. IKEA makes it bearable, providing inexpensive diapers, baby food, and day care services for parents who want some quality shopping time. Can you imagine letting Kmart babysit for you?

- *Tasty.* I go just for the Swedish meatballs. The restaurant is so good (and cheap) that lunch is a highlight.

- *Mystery.* Every product name is Swedish. The names are so quirky that there are websites dedicated to decoding them. Need a Jerker, a Skänka, or some Skydd?

- *Good products.* You know what you're getting when you buy from IKEA. Cool, cheap stuff. It's pretty much a sure thing. It's worth your time and worth telling your friends about.

Action Plan: Finding Your Topics

Here's the bad news for good marketers: The better you are at writing great marketing copy, the worse you're going to be at finding great word of mouth topics.

Why? Because real people don't repeat marketing copy. And it's hard for great copywriters to stop thinking about great copy. Remember this rule: If it looks great in a press release, brochure, or advertisement—it's an awful word of mouth topic.

But don't worry. It just takes a little bit of practice (and a lot of flexibility) to stop thinking about slogans and start thinking about repeatable, portable word of mouth topics.

Use the following worksheets to get started. (You can download printable versions at *www.wordofmouthbook.com*, but I recommend that you buy multiple copies of this book instead.)

The first exercise will help you ask the tough questions about your products. Are they really buzzworthy? Who would tell a friend? What can we change/add/fix to get people talking?

The second exercise will help you start thinking creatively about word of mouth topics that are a little more out there. Have fun with this—it's an exercise best done with beer and/or caffeine.

New Topics Worksheet

Is your product buzzworthy?
Ask the tough questions until you get a definite YES!

PRODUCT:_____

ASK	YOUR PLAN
Would anyone tell a friend? (No. Add something! Maybe. Not good enough! Yes! How do we feature it?)	
What would they say? (This is your WOM topic.)	
Who would they tell? (Does the topic start many conversations?)	
How could they tell more people? (Make it easy to tell five people instead of one.)	

Topics Brainstorming Exercise

Speed exercise: Try to see how many topics you
can find for one type of talker for a single product.
This is about crazy ideas, so get creative!

TALKER: _____

PRODUCT: _____

YOUR PLAN

1.	
2.	
3.	
4.	
5.	
6.	
7.	
8.	
9.	
10.	
11.	
12.	
13.	
14.	
15.	

TOOLS: HOW CAN YOU HELP THE MESSAGE TRAVEL?

Your Job: Make It Easier for the Message to Spread

Word of mouth is powerful, but it doesn't go on forever. When people talk to each other, the conversation only travels a short distance.

Word of mouth gets much, much more powerful when you help it along.

It's nice when someone tells a friend about you—it's nicer when they post an online review that everyone sees. It's nice when someone shares a coupon that you give them—it's nicer when they email that coupon to 50 friends.

Once you've identified your talkers and have a topic you want them to talk about, it's time to figure out everything you can do to accelerate the process. The tools we discuss here are some of the many things you can use to help get the message out.

Remember our original definition: Give people a reason to talk about your stuff and *make it easier for the conversation to take place.* That's what the tools are all about.

LEGO discovered something interesting: Grownups like to play with LEGOs, too. These fans were relatively quiet and inactive—until LEGO put up a message board where all of them could get together, talk about their hobby, and share ideas. As you can imagine, word of mouth took off like crazy. The tool was a message board that super-charged an existing, low-level conversation. The community became active, involved, and connected—and it turns out that adults have a lot more money to spend than toddlers.

Tools don't have to be complicated. One of the lost word of mouth classics is the free postcards that used to be in every hotel room. A postcard is just a little advertisement for your hotel. Sending that postcard home used to be a ritual. It was a great tool, a simple way to make it easier for people to tell their friends. A postcard is word of mouth perfection.

Fast-Moving Waters

The key concepts to keep in mind with tools are *speed* and *portability.*

Think of your topic as a drop of oil on a fast-moving river. The moment it touches the surface, it spreads far and wide in a high-speed rush. Things like viral emails, popular blogs, and product review sites are examples of major currents that you want to ride. These are the tools that drive accelerated word of mouth today.

Here's a simple suggestion: Put your latest topic in the bottom of all your outgoing emails. Do it for the whole company. You might send 50 to 500 emails each week. Your entire office sends many times more—and always to people who are actively engaged with your company. Think of your email signature as an idea-insertion vehicle. Change the message once a month and you have a powerful tool to get portable topics moving.

The Internet Is Your Most Powerful Tool

Much of this section will talk about how to use the internet to accelerate word of mouth. The most efficient and effective tools are online. As I've pointed out, 80 percent of word of mouth happens offline, and you should focus on the talkers, topics, and taking part that occur in the real world. But when it comes to spreading your messages faster and farther, the internet is the communication engine. Just remember that online tools spark conversations that may begin on the internet but don't necessarily end there.

Three Must-Use Word of Mouth Marketing Tools

Grab a pencil. Write this down.

If you do nothing else I recommend, if you ignore the rest of this book, put these three things on your to-do list. They will get you more word of mouth than anything:

1. Ask people to spread the word.

2. Put everything in an email.

3. Put a tell-a-friend link on every page of your website.

These tools are free, they are easy, and they are the most effective ways to turn a single recommendation into powerful word of mouth.

Ask People to Spread the Word

Sometimes all you need to do is ask.

The first and foremost tool for creating word of mouth is the easiest and most obvious: asking nicely. Most people won't talk until you ask them to. So ask often and ask everywhere.

The challenge isn't necessarily finding talkers; it's triggering the talking action. Often the implied compliment of asking customers to help is what starts them down the road to becoming talkers. Remember that inviting your talkers to spread the word is a way of conferring status and making them insiders.

The term for this is a *call to action*. These are visual and verbal requests for people to do something. Weave calls to action into everything you do. Use the power of suggestion. It works. Here are some ideas:

- Put the words "Tell a friend," "Pass it on," or something like that all over your website. (It doesn't matter if they click on them. The visual reminder puts the idea in their heads.)

- Put these words in every email, too.

- Train your sales staff to end each sale with a thank you and a friendly, "Don't forget to tell your friends."

- Put a request on the receipt.

- Put a sign on the door.

- Send a reminder email after each online order.

Before my organization's annual conference, we sent a message to every one of our members, asking them to email their clients and associates about the conference. We also asked them to post a reminder to their blogs and newsletters. Each recipient was given a unique "secret" discount code, which made them look good when they passed it along. The codes were fun, and they encouraged sharing. (Company XYZ's secret code was "weloveXYZ.")

Volunteers need to be asked to volunteer. Most people won't step up on their own. Nonprofit organizations are good at doing this. They know that raising money or getting converts is the second step, after asking a bunch of talkers to go out and spread the word.

Asking is easy, but most companies forget to do it.

Put It in an Email

Put it in an email. Put it in an email. Put *everything* in an email.

Email is the fastest, most portable, most effective word of mouth tool ever invented. Email is freedom for ideas to move. When you put a topic in an email, you are making it sharable.

Take everything you are doing and email it to someone. Create an email newsletter so you can send topics to lots of people. Let talkers sign up for your email lists on your home page.

> The key concepts to keep in mind with tools are speed and portability.

A paper coupon is a single-user promotion. An email coupon can bring in thousands of new people through word of mouth.

If you really want an email to take off, use these essential strategies for high-velocity email:

- *Make sure it's forwardable.* Far too many overdesigned emails fall apart when forwarded, with broken graphics and links. Send it to yourself on different accounts and computers, and make sure it looks great when passed along.

- *Write it for the second recipient.* Make sure that your email makes sense to pass-along readers who get it from a friend. They may not know who you are. Add sections for "About the Company," "About This Newsletter," and anything else that tells your exciting story to someone who is seeing you for the first time.

- *Capture new talkers.* Every email should have sign-up instructions right in the message. Don't expect secondhand recipients to go to your site and search for how to get on the list. Grab them while they are hot and ready to act.

- *Tell recipients to tell a friend.* Put a big, bold call to action right at the top. Remember, talkers talk when you ask them to. Include a link to a tell-a-friend form right in the message.

These great email tricks are also worth a try:

- *Be funny.* Put something amusing at the end of every message just to get it forwarded. The last story of my newsletter is always funny, often weird, and rarely related to the rest of the message. People love to pass along odd stuff, so the fun bit causes the forwarding, and the marketing messages go along for the ride.

- *Tell readers NOT to forward the message.* Works every time. My most-forwarded messages all start with the phrase "PRIVATE: DO NOT FORWARD."

Tell-a-Friend Forms

Put a tell-a-friend form or link on every page of your website.

It can be a little icon or link that says "tell a friend" or "email this page" or whatever. You can get fancy and add a little form right on the page for people to fill out.

Think about it. Someone is on your website, looking at something that you are selling—and they feel the urge to tell someone else. *Make it easy.* That person is about to advertise for you, for free, with their personal endorsement. Or they need to ask someone a question before they buy. Or they just like what they see. Do whatever it takes to let that word of mouth happen.

A desire to make a referral is a magic moment. Make sure the magic is only one click away. Plus, this reinforces the "just ask" principle.

Don't let your webmaster get in the way or tell you that this is too complicated or expensive. You can use one of many low-cost or free plug-ins for your website to have this installed in less than one hour. Here are the secrets to creating effective referral forms:

- *Make it fast.* Design a form that can be filled out in less than 15 seconds. Get rid of optional fields, passwords, or anything that gets in the way of the referral.

- *Ask for several referrals.* Be sure to explicitly ask users to forward the message to multiple friends. The more you ask, the more you get. Design the form so it's easy to add lots of names without confusion.

- *Use the sender's name.* When you deliver the message, make sure it is from the referrer, not your website. The recipient isn't expecting mail from you and might delete it. The recipient will open a message from a friend.

- *Include a personal message.* Let the sender add text to the message. The referral is far more powerful when the talker gets to put it in her own words.

- *Make it reforwardable.* Take a look at the message that recipients get. Is that message a ready-to-go viral email, or is it some cryptic link? Follow the advice above for creating a message that will get shared.

- *Protect privacy.* And brag about it. Be clear and explicit that you respect the privacy of the senders and recipients using the form and that you won't use their emails for any other purpose (and stick to what you promise). Usage will skyrocket when you do this.

Multiply the Sharing

It's a shame if a talker only talks to one person.

Expand the power of your talkers by making it easier for them to share with more than one person at a time. Add extra lines for more recipients on your tell-a-friend forms. Be sure that your talkers have all the brochures and freebies they want. Always ask for two referrals instead of one. Don't send one copy of your book or product to be reviewed—send enough for the entire office. That will get everyone to try it and to talk about it.

Tools are all about making it easier for the conversation to take place.

When Seth Godin published a compilation of essays called *The Big Moo*, he primed the pump before its official publication date by offering prerelease copies for $2 each. But the catch was, you had to buy a case of 50. He made the offer to people he knew would talk up the book and pass it along to other interested talkers. The proceeds from this prepublication sale went to charity, and Godin put 10,000 copies of the book in the hands of 200 of his best talkers.

Always look for other ways to add multipliers to your word of mouth tools. A printed coupon should include a second one to hand to a friend. Give out Post-it Notes instead of flyers, because each pack gets shared with 50 people. Give out three free samples instead of one. Add "bring a guest" to any private invitation.

Potbelly Sandwich Works is a fantastic sandwich chain in Chicago that is just starting to go national. The way they get people talking in each new market is a fantastic demonstration of pure offline word of mouth.

Case Study:
Potbelly—
Multiply the Talk

When they opened their first stores in Austin, Potbelly's Laura Berrones came up with the idea of renting a postal mailing list of people who had moved to Austin from Chicago. The company mailed each of them a single-page, hand-signed, hand-addressed letter that said:

> *Congrats on your recent move! I hope you are settling in and enjoying Austin. But I must ask, are you at all homesick? ...We are thrilled to bring you a taste of home by opening a Potbelly Sandwich Works in Austin. Now you can finally introduce your friends and coworkers to that quirky sandwich joint you've been talking about so much. Enclosed you'll find ten free sandwich tickets, our gift to you, to help you share the Potbelly love with your friends.*

The genius part: the ten free sandwiches. Had it been one free sandwich, each recipient would have eaten it. With ten coupons, they walk around their offices or dorms asking everyone if they want to come to lunch, telling everyone how great Potbelly is. You turn a customer into a talker—a talker who you've helped look cool for buying lunch for the whole crew.

Those ten tickets are a multiplier, something that turns a single word of mouth recommendation into many recommendations. (Anyone who got the letter could also sign up to be on the VIP email list, which included an invitation to a private opening-day party. Remember, you need to do more than just find your talkers—you need a way to communicate with them.)

Twofers

The classic "two for the price of one" offer is all about word of mouth. This works best with things that need a second person present, like movie tickets (it's hard to sit in two seats at the same time). You get bonus word of mouth when the talker is asking around, looking for that friend to share it with.

Costco sometimes offers a free membership for a friend when a current member renews. It's a great idea. The current member gets the status of setting up her friend with a great deal, and she spreads word of mouth while she is looking for someone to give it to. Costco makes up the cost on the renewal of the friend the next year (and then she brings a friend, too).

The Week magazine sent me a subscription card that offered a free subscription for a friend if we signed up at the same time. I'd been meaning to subscribe, so the offer gave me the impetus I needed to do it, plus a real reason to talk about *The Week* to my friends. I talked to four people in the office before one took the freebie. The magazine got good word of mouth and at least two new subscribers.

Make Your Pages Super-Viral

Make it really, really easy for users to share your web pages. You can do so much more than just the standard tell-a-friend form. Design the entire page to encourage word of mouth.

YouTube beat out 30 identical competitors to become the biggest video-sharing site. The secret? It is really good at asking people to email their friends and makes it incredibly easy. Every page has many ways to share a video, including:

- A "Share" link
- HTML code ready to paste right into your own website
- Links that can automatically send the video to your social network accounts without leaving YouTube

- Another "Share" link that fills the screen after you watch the video

- A super-simple form for sharing that takes less than three seconds to use

- Saving the email addresses of people you send to so you can send to them again (This is powerful. If you send a video to your mom the first time, and your sister the second time, both email addresses are waiting to be used again without retyping. The next time you go to share a video with your dad, there's good chance that you'll also send it to mom and sis, because their emails are right there.)

Build Word of Mouth into Your Product

Look for ways to build word of mouth right into your stuff. The challenge: Add qualities or features that make spreading the word an automatic result of using the product.

The creation of Hotmail is a classic story of word of mouth marketing. In 18 months, the company went from zero to more than eight million users, then was sold for $400 million, with little more promotion than word of mouth. The secret? Every email had a little link at the bottom that said "Get Your Free Email from Hotmail." Hotmail is what we would call a pure viral product—there is no way to use the product without also spreading word of mouth about it.

For a generation, what was the first thing you did with a Polaroid photo? You gave it to a friend. Polaroid made its stuff even more portable when it came up with film that was sticky on the back. Photos so ready to travel that you can stick them to people, bikes, and cars.

It won't work for everything, but try to find features that make using your product and sharing your product part of the same process.

Look for Network Effects

If you had the only fax machine in the world, it would be useless. If a few people have them it's okay, but they get exponentially more useful as more people get them. That's the network effect. You've seen it for phones, faxes, email, instant messaging, and most new communication technologies. Network effects put out giant waves of word of mouth.

The latest example of this is Skype, an internet-only phone service that is mostly used for calling other Skype users. You need your friends to have an account if you want to call them with it, so you bug them and talk about its benefits. Other internet phone services don't have the same power of network-effect word of mouth, because their phones make calls to regular phone lines. There's no reason to talk to your friends about it, because it doesn't matter to you whether they use it.

Think about calling circles, buddy lists, team discounts, and any other reason a customer would benefit when her friends use your product, too.

Stuff to Share

Don't expect anyone to remember to talk about you. Put something in their hands that reminds them, motivates them, and makes them look good.

Give them stuff to share.

Electronic Pass-Alongs

Create an entire package of electronic cut-and-paste pass-alongs. Include everything talkers might need if they were going to post something about you on the internet. At a minimum, you need:

- Logos, banner ads, and icons. Make them in all the standard sizes so they will fit wherever someone wants to paste them.
- Sample text in different styles and lengths.
- Ready-to-forward email messages.

You get even more word of mouth when you create richer content. More interesting items are more likely to get forwarded. Try sounds, animations, ecards, and cut-and-paste code that inserts the promotion right into web pages. This ready-to-insert web content is called a "widget."

The more you give to your talkers, the easier it is for them to talk. Just as important, you gain a little bit of control over the content and look of the message when you give them the words and images.

When announcing a new project, create a special email that asks your talkers to help you spread the word. The top of the message should have an introduction and explanation, along with some ready-to-paste images and sample text. The bottom of the message should be a ready-to-forward email promotion, already mail-merged with the talker's name. All they need to do is trim off the top and forward it.

Handouts and Takeaways

Never let somebody walk out of your store empty-handed.

Remember when smokers roamed free in restaurants, bars, and other public places? Every restaurant gave away matchbooks with its logo on the cover. They were a useful little takeaway that reminded the customer of the business every time he lit up—and they were passed along. Well, with smoking on the decline, what replaces the matchbook? Think of little doodads your customers could pick up and use. Then slap your name and your topic all over them.

Give the shopper something to stuff in her pocket and show to a friend, a spouse, a coworker. Pens, calendars, and magnets are some of the many things you can hand out for free to keep the conversation going. At the very least, have business cards or pocket-sized flyers by the cash register.

These handouts have two simple functions. They remind the talker to talk (when they get taken out of the pocket or shopping bag later), and they give talkers something to talk about.

They are conversation starters.

If you sell expensive or complicated products, put little info flyers next to each item on display. A sheet of paper with product specifications is also a tool that a shopper can take home and show someone. It helps the shopper make a purchase decision—but it also allows the product and store to get talked about more easily to someone new.

If I ran a restaurant, I'd give six extra desserts to anyone headed back to the office after lunch. One dessert would get eaten, but six will get the person walking around the office trying to give them away, talking about how great your restaurant is.

Think about that simple thing you can hand to your talkers to remind them to talk.

Stuff the Package

If your company sells products via catalog or the web, you don't have face-to-face contact with your customers, and your customers don't rub elbows in your store.

How do you turn those buyers into talkers?

You stuff the box with word of mouth tools.

The package that you ship is a great word of mouth opportunity—and you can put plenty in there without adding any postage expense. Think of all the cool stuff you could throw in that might get your customers talking about you.

At the very least, put the following in every package that you ship: three coupons to share with friends, three catalogs or flyers, and three samples of something. Put the tools to make a referral right in the customer's hands. It's a great time to do it. They are excited about having just received their new product, and they are probably primed to become talkers.

Even better, surprise them with something fun. A handwritten thank-you will blow them away. Include a nice case for the product. When I buy laminating supplies by mail, I find a bag of M&Ms in every order. It's just unusual enough that I tell people about it, and the office interns tell their friends at other companies (after stealing my candy).

Honeymoon Kit

Remember those brand-new customers who may be your most prolific (but short-term) talkers? You need a fast-acting tool to turn them on before they fade away.

Capture that new-customer enthusiasm during the honeymoon period by creating a honeymoon kit that gives them everything they need to start talking. Fill it with the same pass-along items mentioned above. Hand them an envelope with a welcome letter and some coupons to share.

Every customer who buys from Dale and Thomas Popcorn can immediately send a free sample to anyone else. New customers are talking before their order even ships. New members of Crunch gym are handed guest passes so they can bring their friends.

For more complex products, you can create an entire welcome experience. Include training materials, logos to put on websites, useful documents, and some fun items, too. Include a survey that asks for the names of other people you should be talking to at the recipient's company.

Go ahead and ask your new customer to give you a referral. People who just decided to do business with you will want to reinforce that decision by getting their friends involved. Plus, you flatter them and make them feel included in your family when you ask for help.

Build It to Be Stolen

Market research company eMarketer is a master of the concept of cut-and-paste word of mouth. Their email newsletters and website are full of fantastic graphs and charts. Each image is perfectly sized to paste right into a report or PowerPoint. It also is designed so you can't help but see that it's from eMarketer.

The word of mouth power of this technique is amazing. Every day, executives across the country are showing off eMarketer in meetings, speeches, and memos. Massive word of mouth. eMarketer keeps it going with fresh new topics (ready-to-copy charts) every week. Why advertise when people will show you off for free?

What can you do to make your stuff easier to steal and share?

Samples and Seeding

Here's something so obvious that most people miss it: People don't talk about things that they have never seen or tried. (Okay, some people do, but who listens to them?)

You need to get samples of your products into your talkers' hands to kick off the conversation.

The legend of the launch of Post-it Notes is a wonderful word of mouth story. At first, the product was going nowhere, because nobody had seen these things or knew what to do with them (or even knew to ask for them). So the secretary of the CEO of 3M started using them on documents sent to executives around the country and sent samples to the secretaries of other Fortune 500 CEOs. Needless to say, they used them, they shared them, and the rest is history. (Post-its have great built-in word of mouth qualities because you usually share them when you use them.)

There's nothing new about the idea of free samples. Marketers have been using them forever. But there is a specific word of mouth marketing application of the technique. The goal is to get samples into the hands of the most likely talkers. It's not about giving stuff away to potential customers; it's about getting the product in the hands of potential word of mouth advocates. The term that's often used for this is *seeding*—you are planting the seed of a conversation.

> **The first and foremost tool for creating word of mouth is the easiest and most obvious: asking nicely.**

If you've got a good list of talkers, you can mail them something. You can also keep samples handy for those especially chatty customers when they come into the store. When Coca-Cola launched Coke Zero, they sent a case home with every employee. That's a lot of free samples and a lot of conversations.

The trick is to know where your talkers are. Public venues tend to attract connected talkers—concerts, sporting events, bars, and any place social people gather. It may be a mass event like a baseball game, or it may be a small but influential business function.

Trade shows are a great place to reach highly concentrated talker groups. Your sample doesn't need to match the theme of the event— it just needs to be something that these folks will take home to show their friends.

Tylenol has a fantastic program in which they sponsor skateboarding competitions. They know that the participants are highly social, very connected talkers. And these kids seriously need painkillers. These talkers are also very resistant to advertising and would probably turn against marketers who blatantly try to sell to them. So Tylenol does something very clever: It pays to support the events, but it doesn't put up any signs or logos. It just provides free painkillers and lets the word spread naturally. The company knows that it has found the right talkers—and those talkers know who's providing the cash. The gratitude spreads through word of mouth.

The Power of Swag

Never underestimate the power of swag—free hats, shirts, bags, toys, or anything with company logos on it.

While it's true there is a guy somewhere who will sell you advertising space on his forehead, most of us will never find anyone who would accept any amount of money to be a human billboard. Yet people will display your logo every day on a hat or shirt.

If people identify with your brand and love your stuff, wearing or carrying your logo around is a way to support you. Sometimes it's unintentional. I carried around a PayPal backpack for an entire year. (It's a nice bag.) I don't use PayPal often, but I displayed the company's logo at every speech I delivered, in front of hundreds of people each time.

Every item with your logo becomes a word of mouth generator when it's worn by a real person. It starts conversations and gets people asking about it. And precisely because it's not paid advertising but a personal expression, the message is authentic and credible, a recommendation instead of a commercial.

Give away lots of free stuff.

Conversation Triggers

Create simple items that prompt a word of mouth conversation. Many talkers won't start a conversation about you but will sing your praises if anyone else mentions you. So do things that get you mentioned.

Word of mouth triggers are little, visible objects that cause people to ask about you. A framed certificate for customers to display in their offices will trigger a "what is that?" from their visitors.

I've taken every business card that I've received in the past ten years, glued my logo to the back, used a laminator to turn it into a luggage tag, and mailed it back to the person I just met. I'll bet that at least 5,000 people have my logo on their briefcase or suitcase. When they meet each other, they talk about my company. That's a lot of word of mouth.

An organization called the Association Forum was recruiting new members. Membership in an association isn't one of those things that just pops up in everyday conversations. So they made bobblehead dolls to send to their current members, who were thrilled to get the cool toy. The next time a coworker noticed the doll sitting on a member's desk, it prompted an instant word of mouth conversation. Sales jumped.

Sharable Advertising

Your advertising is a great word of mouth topic—but it's hard to send a TV spot to a friend. After you run any sort of paid ad, be sure to make a word of mouth version. Post PDFs of print ads on your website. Upload TV spots to YouTube. Put audio files on your blog.

You've already paid to run the ad, now let your fans share it again for free.

Blogs

In the context of word of mouth marketing, here's why blogs matter: They are a tool for extending and accelerating the conversation. Starting one is a long-term commitment, but it's not hard to do. The payoff is worth it.

This section isn't about how to blog. Plenty of other books cover that. This is about how blogs create word of mouth.

Blogs Make Messages Portable

Blogs are all about linking, sharing, and connecting.

Put a topic on a blog, and it's instantly ready for word of mouth. Every blog post has instructions for how to link to it and how to email it, and provides credit and recognition for those who do.

This is why they have been so successful: A story on a blog gets picked up by other blogs, and visitors get linked back and forth between them. This turns anything you write into a viral message the moment it's posted. On top of that, blog entries show up very prominently in search engines.

Blogs Create New Topics

Your company probably has a lot to say and a lot to share. But you can't issue a press release every day.

A blog is the tool that lets you put out fresh ideas and information. It is designed for small, frequent updates—almost like having your own news wire. It's the perfect way to keep your talkers fed with new topics and ideas. Everything you post gives people something new to talk about.

Blogs Provide a Place
for the Conversation to Happen

Talkers need other people to talk to. A blog becomes the location of that conversation. It brings everyone together, it connects the conversation to similar ones on other blogs, and it provides a place to go when someone wants to talk. The blog provides critical mass that takes conversations to the next level.

Just look at the comments on a blog. All those little responses represent talkers who wanted to express their opinions. The blog makes it possible, and it is the tool that shares that conversation with other readers.

Blogging Builds Credibility

Bloggers respect bloggers. You can't just show up and expect everyone to talk about you, any more than you can show up at a party and expect to be the center of attention. You've gotta earn it.

Start blogging now, so you have time to build relationships and credibility before you need it. You want to become a known quantity and a part of the conversation. That way, when you are ready to interact with blogs, you are seen as a member of the community instead of a crass marketer looking for shameless publicity.

Online Communities and Social Media

Online communities, forums, and social networks are the high-energy homes of word of mouth. Discussions about products and services start, spread, and stay there permanently. These are powerful tools that you need to learn to work with.

It doesn't matter what you are selling. Someone has created an online community for your industry. These forums are active and very focused, sometimes focused on exactly what you do.

I was shopping for picture frames online and found dozens of stores that carried pretty much the same thing. But it only took one glowing review on a message board for photographers about a particular store's reliable shipping to make my decision. I trusted the genuine word of mouth from someone I'd never met. And I found it in a place no traditional marketer would consider relevant.

Your customers are doing the same research about you.

Create Your Own Community

You can create a community or forum for your fans in just a few minutes. It doesn't matter if you do it on a third-party site or on your own page. Just go wherever it would be easiest for your talkers to participate.

You can use free web software to add a forum to your site, create a group on a social network, or use one of the many (often free) community-hosting websites.

It creates an instant home for your talkers. As soon as you put it up you'll find all sorts of talkers coming out of the woodwork to participate. When they do, the community creates a public word of mouth archive to attract future discussions.

We've already discussed what LEGO and Intuit have done. It works just as well for small businesses. MusicToyz.com is a web store for guitar junkies. It's a one-man operation that could never afford a traditional advertising campaign. But its online forum is the best place to talk about eclectic, electric guitar gear. The last time I looked, it had 4,000 registered users, 65 people online at once, and more than 250,000 messages posted. All that action is a written record of the word of mouth conversation. It grabs shoppers off the search engines and funnels them right into the store.

Turning Social Sites into Word of Mouth Tools

No word of mouth tool has as much potential for scale and reach as social media. You've hit the big time if you can get your stuff picked up in the conversation stream. It's just a matter of getting involved. And, of course, doing it ethically. Pay close attention to the honesty rules in chapter 1.

These sites are hotbeds of word of mouth. Much of the everyday conversation about products and services has moved there, where it has been linked to, connected, and accelerated. It's too big to ignore.

You don't need to be the first company to pioneer a new social community. There's a lot of pressure to be all over the next new thing. Don't worry about it. Wait until it's clear that the site is going to be around and that your customers will actually use it. Follow your customers into new sites instead of expecting them to follow you.

The good news is that participation is open, easy, and free. Here's how to start:

Create Profiles and Pages

All of the social sites let you set up your own account, with your own pages, identities, and topics of conversation. Do this on any site where your customers might be participating. Once you have a page, you have something for fans and friends to link to. Having a presence causes the conversation to happen.

Each site has its own audience with a different style of communicating, and each one spreads word of mouth to a different audience. Learn how each one works and then get in there.

Be Social-Media Friendly

Many of the connections and links on social media websites are automated. If you create your pages the right way, you'll get included in the linking. Most of the sites use something called tags, which are little bits of text that identify your web pages. Learn to tag, because it will instantly connect your pages to the word of mouth conversation. (This is an important tool, but too complicated to explain in this book. Do a little research—it's a huge, free word of mouth opportunity.)

Ask Your Talkers to Connect to You

You can be sure that a significant number of your talkers are already participating in these communities and social networks. In fact, it is probably where they are already doing some of their talking about you. Don't sit back and hope to get noticed. Your success on these sites is a function of how many connections you have, so reach out to your talkers, tell them that you're there, and ask them to connect their pages to yours or join your groups.

Exclusivity, Secrets, and Surprises

Exclusivity and participation are powerful word of mouth tools. They turn mildly interested people into rabid fans.

When you engage people in a product and make them feel as though it is *their* product, it translates directly into a desire to talk about it. Groupies are promoters—and all they want is a taste of what it's like to be the rock star. Look for ways to put specialness, exclusivity, and fun into being a talker.

Remember the Pepsi Challenge? Coke drinkers who chose Pepsi were surprised, Pepsi drinkers were self-congratulatory—and everyone was spreading word of mouth about Pepsi.

Make It Exclusive

Deep down inside, we all like to feel special. It's a strong motivator for word of mouth conversations. Many people are more likely to talk about a product if they have some kind of insider access or privileged status.

This is one of the reasons that the talker programs we discussed earlier work so well. When you call someone an ambassador, a VIP, or a member of the club, you're making them feel special. Every time they tell someone about your stuff, they are also reinforcing their status.

It works with any kind of status. When Google launched Gmail, its free email service, it made the product entirely word of mouth driven. In fact, the company made it a privilege to be allowed to share the product. The only way to get an account was if a friend invited you. First, you would receive an invitation from a friend (you feel special!). Once you were signed up, you got a limited number of invitations to send to your friends (now you're important!). In fact, for more than two years, you couldn't sign up for the service unless you got a referral from a friend. What a great way to lock in the exclusivity topic.

Keep It Secret

It's human nature to want to share a secret. You should use the power of gossip to encourage word of mouth.

Instead of announcing your topics to your talkers—try hiding them. Make people work to dig them up. The fun of the hunt and the excitement of discovery are worth talking about. When talkers discover the secret benefit, they are that much more likely to want to blab the secret to everyone they know.

Restaurants can offer a special dish that only insiders know about. Have the waiter casually mention it to each new customer, on the sly. I bet they'll go right out and spread a little word of mouth about the delicious secret that they discovered. Some restaurants have set up a private phone number so regular customers can always get a reservation.

Stores can offer a product or add-on that isn't apparent to regular shoppers. Maybe special gift wrapping, a unique flavor, or a delivery service. Let the word spread that you have this available for people who ask.

Video games and DVDs have used this trick for years. They are full of what are called "Easter eggs," which are fun displays that are only revealed if you know the secret code. Conversation about where to find these surprises fills message boards and keeps people talking about the products.

Give Sneak Previews

Everyone wants to be a movie reviewer and get invited to exciting premieres. We like to see things first. Why? Because we feel special when we tell our friends.

The sneak preview is one of the most reliable word of mouth tools. The desire to get a preview is directly tied to the desire to talk about what you just saw.

Think of talkers as your advance team. Always give them an early taste of your next new thing. They will pay you back by talking to everyone and building demand before the product is even available.

Give them an advance look to keep them excited and enough information to look smart to the people they're talking to. Keep it simple. Create an email list for insiders with upcoming offers and developments.

Retailers: Offer private shopping hours for your talkers the night before new products are available to the public. Restaurants: Host a preview meal to show off your new menu or chef. Car dealers: Invite your talkers in for a test drive of new cars before anyone even knows that they have arrived. Software companies: Send prerelease versions of software to anyone active on a related message board.

Cell phone companies have started sending new models not just to the big electronics publications but to hundreds of bloggers. That's a radical change. New models used to be top secret, with the manufacturers suing anyone who leaked the design. Now, leaks are a word of mouth motivator. (You should send out tester versions of new products to your fans, too.)

Let Your Talkers Build the Product

Talkers who get to see an early version of a product are usually eager to talk about it. When you let them participate, they become committed to its success and locked in as part of the team.

Google always has dozens of new products in development—and you could play with them through Google Labs. Anyone could try a product in development, suggest features, and discuss it online. That early participation guaranteed that all sorts of people were aware of the product, involved, and ready to spread word of mouth when it launched. It's since been shut down, but it was great while it lasted.

The software industry has turned beta tests into immense word of mouth programs. Originally, beta tests were designed to get real users to debug products. These days, the programs are so huge, the word of mouth function is just as important. Millions of people tested the 2007 versions of Windows and Microsoft Office. Each one of these testers is now an insider, with an emotional interest in the success of the platform. People rarely criticize a product that they helped build.

Testimonials and Customer Reviews

Word of mouth is so effective because of the natural credibility that comes from real people with no profit or agenda tied to their recommendations. It's those "people like us" whom we look for and listen to.

Recommendations, testimonials, and thank you letters from those real people are great, but they are often invisible to potential customers. A testimonial sent to you in a private letter or email never reaches anyone else.

You've got a talker and you've got a topic. Now you need a tool, because the recommendation won't get to a new reader without your help.

Promote Positive Testimonials

Testimonials are nice to receive. But they have a much greater impact when you actively manage them. Don't just pile up that good feedback in a desk drawer—turn it into a word of mouth tool. The steps are simple:

1. *Ask for testimonials.* Most customers are glad to give them. But they won't think to do it without a little prompting. It's perfectly fine to ask any customer, "Would you mind giving me a short recommendation?" You should also have a form on your website where anyone can submit feedback of any sort. If the customer isn't sure what to say, feel free to suggest something. Just be careful not to cross the line by asking him to say something that he doesn't believe (the Honesty of Opinion rule applies here).

2. *Get permission to share.* Don't forget to ask for permission to use the testimonial in your marketing material. It will be very embarrassing if you use a testimonial and the recommender later denies having made it or has left her job. You'll need the written record to prove that you had permission to mention

the person and the company. You don't need a formal contract, but do get an explicit okay in writing or in email. The easiest thing to do is add a check box to a form on the website. When someone sends you a nice email or an unsolicited compliment, you should also feel free to email them back for permission. I frequently send a note that says something like, "Thanks for the kind words. May I quote you in our marketing materials?"

3. *Put it all on your website.* This is the point! Show off all those great recommendations. Put the word of mouth out there where everyone will see it.

4. *Link to compliments already on the web.* Now that you've got a page full of positive word of mouth, go surfing for anything else online. You'll find a ton on blogs. Link to each of these. As long as it's posted publicly, you don't need explicit permission.

Work with Customer Review Sites

You obviously want to get good reviews wherever your products are discussed. But you also need a large number of reviews.

When people scan the reviews for your stuff, they are looking for two things. First, are the reviews good? Second, how many people have bothered to review you?

There's power in numbers. The quantity of reviews is a measure of how word-of-mouth-worthy your stuff is. If people are reviewing your products—good, bad, or mixed—you have a conversation you can work with. If no one is reviewing your products, it signals to the shopper that your stuff isn't even worth considering. Nobody is excited about it one way or the other. In the absence of reviews, many shoppers will assume the worst and look for a more popular product.

Sometimes you have to ask people to post reviews. Or do what eBay and others have done: Build a request for a review into the shopping transaction. Try putting a slip of paper into the box you ship. When you send an email receipt, include a link to the major sites that review you.

And remember—no padding the reviews and no employees logging in under fake names. Always be honest.

Capture Passive Word of Mouth

What is a best-seller list? It is passive word of mouth.

Each of those rankings represents an implicit recommendation made by a previous buyer. Those thousands of buyers may not have intentionally planned on engaging in word of mouth, but their collective voice is a powerful form of it.

Put a tell-a-friend form or link on every page of your website.

There are other examples of this. Amazon's "Customers who bought this item also bought..." lists give you the implied recommendations of all those shoppers. iTunes lets you see other people's song lists. My personal favorite is the list of "most emailed stories" from newspapers' websites. It gives you a direct, explicit sense of what people are recommending.

When you tell your customer that "other people bought this," you are turning these passive recommendations into useful word of mouth. When you post your company's best-seller list, you give shoppers an instant sense of what other people are recommending and the confidence to choose based on those recommendations.

Put these lists on your website. Most online shopping carts already have modules for both a "most popular items" list and a "what other customers bought" list. If you're offline, put up a sign or a chalkboard with "Hot Products" or "Customer Favorites."

Don't make it complicated. In bookstores and video stores, the "Staff Favorites" shelf delivers word of mouth from the employees. Add another shelf for customer favorites.

Business-to-Business Word of Mouth

The first question I get asked after almost every speech is: "Does any of this work for business-to-business (BtoB) marketers?"

Yep. It's exactly the same.

Why? Because it's not about the product—it's about the people. The motivations that get people to talk about business-to-consumer products are the same as those that get people to recommend a business-to-business product.

Your talkers are different, the topics change, and you'll use different tools—but it still comes down to the same basic process: Find people who will talk about you, give them something to say, and make it easier for the conversation to take place. Just walk through the Five Ts process and you'll have a great outcome.

A few things are different (but not different enough to change the process):

- BtoB word of mouth programs are often more organized, with a systematic customer referral program and a team dedicated to introducing current customers to new ones.

- Customers are more willing to help, because they often have a closer relationship (even a partnership) with your company.

- Salespeople are often closely involved, coordinating the process of connecting existing customers to prospects.

You're Already Doing It

In fact, most BtoB marketers have been doing word of mouth marketing for years, but it was hidden inside some other sales or marketing process. Do you do any of these things?

- Ask for testimonials
- Ask customers to be references

- Use case studies
- Publish research
- Have user conferences

If the goal of a marketing program is to get a customer to talk to someone, it's actually a word of mouth marketing program. You'll get better results if you pull all these separate actions together and treat them as elements of a single coordinated word of mouth campaign.

Your Customers Are Already Doing It, Too

Here's a really important idea for BtoB marketers: You're part of a small community where all the key people know each other. Your customers are already talking about you when they meet at trade shows and conferences, and they are constantly comparing notes about vendors.

Word of mouth has always been essential for really big-ticket items. Nobody spends $100,000 without checking out a company's word of mouth reputation.

The Best BtoB Word of Mouth Techniques

The best BtoB word of mouth marketing techniques are all fairly simple and inexpensive (like most word of mouth). Look at the marketing you're already doing and rethink it in terms of the big question: How can I make it easier for people to share?

1. *White papers and research*. People love to share articles and data. They get quoted, copied, and forwarded to everyone in the office. When you publish stuff like this, make sure it's sharable. Get rid of the complicated form that people need to fill out to download the paper. It just stops the sharing. (Your salespeople will grumble, but you're trading a few weak leads for widespread word of mouth that attracts better leads.) Even better, replace your fancy PDF with a Word document that can be easily pasted into blogs and newsletters.

2. *Testimonials.* Ask for them everywhere. You should be able to get a positive quote from 90 percent of your customers (except for the few that have a corporate policy against giving them). Display them everywhere. Include testimonials on your home page and in all of your printed sales materials.

   CoffeeCup Software takes it one step further. On their website are names of 100 customers, with a form that lets you ask them any question (not screened by the company). It enables live word of mouth testimonials, and it demonstrates amazing trust by the company and amazing love from their fans.

3. *Email newsletters.* Email newsletters are special—they are the only kind of advertising that people ask for. And they are the single most forwardable word of mouth tool. Create an email newsletter for each of your talker groups, and put the sign-up form on your home page. Even if only a few people sign up, those people are your talkers who are eager for new stuff to talk about.

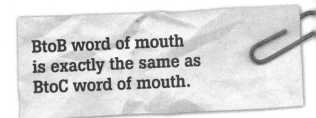

BtoB word of mouth is exactly the same as BtoC word of mouth.

4. *Customer referral programs.* Create a formal program to get existing customers to spread word of mouth to new prospects. Collect testimonials, create video interviews, write case studies, and talk about them on your blog. The secret to making this work is making these talkers feel important. The more you make them look like stars, the more they will talk about you.

5. *Live meetings.* Get your fans together any way you can. Every time they meet each other and meet your team, it increases enthusiasm and gets people talking. It doesn't need to be a formal user conference or a big annual meeting (but those do work well). Have a quarterly barbecue at the office. Invite 20 customers to

dinner every time you travel. Even better, have every employee host a dinner every time they travel. You can meet 1,000 customers a year this way, and create 1,000 happy talkers.

Conferences and Tradeshows

BtoB marketers spend a ton of time at conferences and trade shows. They make speeches and sit on panels. And they usually miss all the best word of mouth opportunities.

When you make a speech, never let anyone leave the room without something to share. You did all that work to prepare, you did a decent job impressing the audience—and then you let them walk away without a word of mouth topic or tool.

Always use a handout (never sales material). I give away bookmarks, a worksheet, and smiley-face buttons. Why? Because these are small things that won't get left behind and will get shared with people back at the office.

Even better, do something surprising. When I speak, I usually bring snacks for the audience. Nobody ever complains about the ten-pound bag of chocolate that I pass around.

When you exhibit at a trade show, a regular booth is never enough. Neither is a silly stunt or a nice handout. Every one of your competitors is doing the exact same thing.

The first step is to push yourself to answer the question: "What would get people to talk about this? Why would someone drag a friend across the exhibit hall to see what we're doing?" Most trade show booths are focused on how to close a sale. Focus on how you can get everyone talking instead.

The second step is to answer: "What will they talk about back at the office?" Attendees will leave the show with a bag full of gifts and flyers—and a blurry memory of their conversation with you. Focus less on how you can get a lead in the booth and more on what is going to cause them to tell everyone about you when they get home. Instead of giving them a gift, offer to mail it (so it starts a conversation a week later, when they are undistracted). Take their picture with a celebrity in the booth, and email it to them in a week. Help it go viral by posting it to a website as an ecard so they can forward it to their friends.

TAKING PART: HOW CAN YOU JOIN THE CONVERSATION?

Your Job: Participate in the Conversation

Most of us don't talk to ourselves. It's just not very interesting. We need someone else to hold up the other end of the conversation to keep it going.

Word of mouth is a dialogue. Someone says something about you, and you answer. If you don't, it rarely goes any further. Your job is to be part of the conversation, and make it come alive. As you know by now, people are talking about you. Wouldn't you rather have them talking with you?

This is so easy to do that you'd be crazy not to do it. Anyone in your company who's interested can step up right now and start participating. Some can listen, some can respond, and some can be out there just monitoring the conversation.

This whole idea is not always easy for traditional marketers (especially spreadsheet-driven number lovers).

Marketing is fundamentally an outbound function: Think of an idea, blast it out there, and hope someone shows up. Most marketing departments aren't organized to accept input from customers or to engage in conversations with them. That's usually customer service's job. Customer service talks to people all day long and, hopefully, tries to make them happy. But customer service is rarely focused on making new sales; and, unfortunately, the average customer service department just wants to get people off the phone as quickly as possible. Marketing and customer service have to learn to work together if word of mouth is going to work for you.

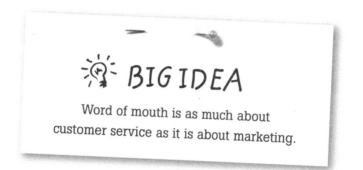

BIG IDEA

Word of mouth is as much about customer service as it is about marketing.

If you want good word of mouth, you'll have to participate. You have to be ready to talk to whomever wants to talk, about whatever they want to talk about.

Many PR-trained executives find this kind of participation difficult because of the inherent lack of control over the situation. It's about learning to respond and participate instead of trying to plant and initiate. It's no longer about managing what other people say but about letting your own words speak for themselves. And it's about earning respect (but not necessarily agreement) from other people out there by showing that you know how to participate the right way.

There are two big risks to ignoring the conversation: Word of mouth dies, or word of mouth goes negative. These days, you stand a serious risk of a word of mouth backlash if you aren't talking with customers when they are talking about you, and you have a greater risk of causing negative word of mouth if you're seen as out of it or snobby.

On the other hand, the more you encourage and participate in word of mouth, the more word of mouth you get. The upside is a valuable, energized, enthusiastic discussion with thousands of talkers who are bringing you loads of free business.

It's an easy decision. Get started!

How to Join the Conversation

Remember this: People want you to participate, as long as you do it as a normal person and not as a corporate spokesperson. That's why everyone is writing all their thoughts on public web pages and asking for comments. They want to hear from you.

Find the Conversation

Every day, people are creating countless messages, blog posts, and emails that are full of word of mouth about businesses. Some of it, we hope, is about you.

As I suggested earlier, someone on your staff should be searching the web every morning for mentions of each of your major products. Make it part of the customer service team's job. Create a list of terms that you need to watch, including brands, product names, and key personnel.

First, use standard search engines to tell you when things are posted on mainstream websites and message boards. Next, use the free specialized search engines that look at blogs and social media sites. They will tell you when something relevant has been posted. These tools are amazingly fast. You often know if something has been posted to a site within seconds. These sites will also let you set up real-time notification to alert you when a new item containing your keywords has been posted.

For real-world conversations, you need to be on the lookout. You probably won't be there when most people are talking about you, so listening for offline word of mouth is a more passive activity. What you can do is be receptive and ready. Pay attention when customers call the company. Be alert wherever you might stumble on a conversation about you.

Reply and Respond

Reply and respond every possible chance you have. Make yourself available to talk to customers directly, anywhere they want to reach you.

There's only one thing you can do that's wrong—fail to participate at all. You really don't have a choice. You must participate if you want any chance of influencing the conversation.

Your ideas and input are welcome as long as they are relevant and in good taste. If bloggers didn't want feedback, they would be writing in paper diaries and stuffing them under their beds.

Thank People Who Say Nice Things about You

Leave a nice comment for the writers when you see a positive mention in a blog or message board. Tell them you appreciate it. Encourage them. You'll be amazed at what a little kindness does for your word of mouth.

You'll get a lot out of this. The original complimenter is more likely to become an active talker. Other people will notice that you're a cool company, and they'll talk about it. On most websites, your comment will automatically link back to your site, bringing you more visitors. And best of all, people will keep saying nice things if they feel warm and fuzzy about you and your stuff.

Fix Problems and Make People Happy

Look for people who have a problem or a complaint. Apologize. Find a way to fix it, or at least offer to.

There is a reason they are complaining in public—they want your attention.

People will fall out of their chairs in shock when you do the right thing. It is so rare for companies to deal nicely with customers that any public, proactive effort becomes an instant word of mouth topic.

When you see a complaint or a gripe, post something like this: "Hi, I'm Andy from XYZ Company. I was reading your blog/message/website and was dismayed to hear that you couldn't get your Floobulator fixed. Try this: _____. Or email me, and I'll hook you up with the right people to take care of it."

You'll do more than make this one talker happy. You'll get every reader of that site gushing about you. Of course, you should be doing the same extraordinary things in your offline customer service, too.

Anyone can make a mistake. How you deal with it determines what the word of mouth will be.

Just Join In

The best possible thing you can do? Be a regular person and a positive contributor.

Every day people are talking about stuff that relates to what you are selling. They care and they are interested. Everyone will be thrilled when someone with your expertise adds to the conversation.

My dad sells something called a TieYak. It's a very clever cable to lock up a kayak (which is harder than you think). It's a small business, and he can't spend much on advertising. But he does have a secret weapon: He knows way too much about kayaks.

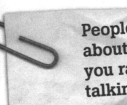

People are talking about you. Wouldn't you rather have them talking with you?

There are 20 or so major message boards about kayaking. Every time he posts a topic, provides helpful advice, or just says hello, his posts automatically contain a link to the TieYak website in his user name. He doesn't need to sell or talk about the product, because people are smart enough to figure it out. His intelligent contributions to the conversation earn the respect that starts the word of mouth about his product.

Case Study:
Levenger—
Anyone Can Do It

Levenger sells sophisticated pens, notepads, and organizers. They also have an impressive number of talkers and a strong presence in the word of mouth conversation.

Every day Ryan Rasmussen, their social media evangelist, went online looking for people talking about Levenger. He answered their questions, helped them use the products, and sometimes uploaded a little video demonstration to YouTube.

He also looked for people talking about fountain pens and personal organization systems, because people who like these topics tend to like Levenger products. When he found these talkers, he commented in the forums, added a suggestion, or shared a useful link. Sometimes he gave out a free sample.

Guess what happened? People started talking about Levenger. They appreciated the attention from the company and they liked the fact that someone from the company took the initiative to contribute to the conversation. There are now thousands of discussions and web pages that mention Levenger.

The best part: Ryan's real job was manager of the Levenger department at a Macy's in Chicago. He wasn't a marketer or a PR person. He went to art school. But he had word of mouth skill #1: passion for the product and a desire to share it.

Find your Ryan. There is someone in your company who would love to do this for you.

The Right People to Take Part

Who should be participating? Anyone!

You don't need a formal word of mouth team. Involve anyone who enjoys being online, has a passion for what you do, and has the time to do it. Don't get too hung up on titles, either. This is a great way to get junior staff involved and give them an opportunity to become stars. I know a lot of successful executives who used their word of mouth smarts and initiative to get noticed and promoted at their companies.

Give your customer service reps access to the internet so they can get online and start looking for problems. Send your administrative assistant online to look for blogs and message boards where people are talking. Get everyone pumped up about the chance to get involved in great word of mouth. For example, gyms should encourage all of their fitness trainers to blog for the company and become online customer advisors. It makes sense—the trainers share the same lifestyle and interests as potential talkers. Many of them are probably blogging anyway.

Do you know if anyone on your staff is blogging? Most of the people who work with you are regularly updating personal social network pages, and more than a few are blogging. If this is new to you, remember that plenty of people do this every day in their personal lives.

Who Should Be Blogging?

Hint: It's not the PR or marketing folks.

Your best blogger will have true enthusiasm for your company and its products and a genuine love for the topic. It is the employee who wears the company shirt on weekends.

Participation never should stem from obligation; it should come from wanting to keep positive word of mouth going and from the knowledge that this is where positive word of mouth gets turned into action. It should be open to anyone who *wants* to do it but no one who *has* to do it.

The bloggers already out there are interested in honest, open dialogue and in being in the know. They'll be able to tell if you're serious about engaging in that kind of exchange.

For your blog to be credible, it's got to be real—honest, passionate, and plain spoken. Blogging is how your company presents a human face, not its business one. Keep the marketing wordsmiths and the lawyers far away from the company blog. Anyone else who can speak honestly and normally should be welcome to do it.

It's Less Risky than You Think

What's the worst thing that could happen? Someone says something inappropriate, does something stupid, or leaks a company secret?

They could do those things anyway. They already have phones and email. Participating in the word of mouth conversation doesn't add new risks, it just changes the location of the conversation.

If something goes wrong, just delete it, apologize, and move on.

Guideposts and Guardrails

Traditional marketing managers and lawyers find this level of free communication really uncomfortable. It's hard enough to give up control of the message and let the customers run with it. It's sometimes harder to free your staff to go off and talk to people without the controls of a formal marketing process.

So do what Intuit does—create what it calls "guideposts and guardrails." Give guidance and training for all interested employees who want to participate in the greater outside conversation. Teach your team the rules of the road and give them the instruction that they need, especially on the ethics rules. Set up strict guardrails that block forbidden behaviors.

Then you just need to let it happen.

If Microsoft can do it, anyone can. This formerly very tight-lipped company with formal marketing controls has opened up and encouraged thousands of employees to start blogging—without supervision or control by the company. And each of those blogs is full of unfiltered comments from the public. The company has seen fantastic improvement in its reputation, consumer trust, and word of mouth, because it showed that it trusts its team and the public to say what they feel.

If you want word of mouth, you'll have to participate.

Getting Started

Use the worksheet on the next page to plan out how you are going to listen and respond. It will help you manage the process. Identify the discussions you should be following and assign someone to listen to each one. Then decide who should be responsible for responding and follow-up.

Daily Participation and Tracking Guide

	Location/site/ tracking tool	Who monitors/ responds?	Results
Real-time tracking	*Example:* Google Alerts	*Example:* Steve/ Customer Service	
Blogs			
Communities			
Social Networks			
Reviews			
Other			

Download this worksheet at *www.wordofmouthbook.com.*

Good Manners

You've heard plenty from me on the importance of honesty and ethics. Taking part is where you are most likely to make a mistake.

Good manners and a little common sense will keep you out of trouble. Step back if you think you're getting into a gray area. There's no good reason to go there (and lots of bad ones).

Never Sell

Taking part does not mean selling. Sticking a shameless sales pitch on a message board or in a blog comment is wrong. It's just like spam. It's hated, and it will embarrass your company.

The purpose of participating is to keep your talkers talking about your topic. It's not to push products. Stick to the discussion topic. Share knowledge, add to the conversation, and make everyone feel appreciated and special.

Follow the Rules

Whether you are at a street fair or on a message board, there are always clear rules. Remember that you are on someone else's turf and you're a guest. Follow the rules wherever you are. Don't litter flyers all over the place. Don't post off-topic comments. Don't aggressively push your product. Just be a good citizen and respect the communities where the conversations are happening.

That may sound restrictive, but it's not. Imagine that on a message board for gardeners, a guy from a lawn mower store breaks the rules and posts a blurb about how great his products are and why they're better than the competition's. He'll probably get kicked off the message board. He'll definitely get attacked by the other posters for being an idiot. Not good word of mouth.

What he should do is talk about lawn problems and answer questions from gardeners who need advice on which products to use.

People will appreciate the contribution and respect his willingness to share and his objectivity. They will also be able to figure out where his store is. That's how you get good word of mouth.

Say Who You Are: The Ten Magic Words

Nothing will turn people off more than you pretending to be something or someone you're not. And don't think for a minute you won't be spotted as a fake if you're out there masquerading as a consumer. As you learned earlier, this kind of shilling is a sure path to embarrassment.

Always disclose aggressively. It's not enough to just post your name. Say where you work and make it very obvious that you have something to gain by being in the conversation.

The best form of disclosure is also the easiest: The Ten Magic Words. Start all of your comments with, "I work for ____, and this is my personal opinion." Not only does this provide simple, clear disclosure, it also protects the company from having to worry about everything said by an employee by making it clear that these aren't official company statements.

There's no need to pretend. Your affiliation with your company gives you *more* credibility, not less. As does your honesty.

Word of Mouth Disclosure: The "Stay Out of Trouble" Checklist

When you're participating in the online conversation, use the following checklist to make sure that you are participating honestly, with proper disclosure. Make it clear to your employees and the agencies you hire that these rules also apply to them. (These best practices were adapted from disclosure guidelines published by SocialMedia.org—a group that I manage. You can learn more at *www.socialmedia.org/disclosure*.)

When communicating in social media on behalf of my company or on topics related to the business of my company, I will:

- ☐ Disclose who I am, whom I work for, and any other relevant affiliations from the very first encounter.
- ☐ Disclose any business/client relationship if I am communicating on behalf of a third party.
- ☐ Provide a means of communicating with me.
- ☐ Proactively ask bloggers to be transparent about their relationship and communications with me.
- ☐ Always be truthful, and never ask anyone to make a deceptive statement for me.
- ☐ Never ask or pay anyone to write a fake endorsement or say something they do not believe.
- ☐ Never use off-topic comments for self-promotional intent.
- ☐ Never take action contrary to the specific boundaries, terms and conditions, and community guidelines set by each website.
- ☐ Not use services or technologies for mass-posting comments.
- ☐ Comply with all laws and regulations regarding disclosure of identity.

On my personal social media accounts, I will:

- ☐ Clearly identify my business affiliation if I write anything related to the business of my employer on personal pages, posts, and comments. (Writing that does not mention work-related topics does not need to mention the employment relationship.)
- ☐ Specifically clarify which posts/comments are my opinions and which are official corporate statements.
- ☐ If I blog anonymously I will not discuss matters related to the business of my employer. If employer-related topics are mentioned, I will disclose my affiliation with the company.

The Power of Making People Happy

Grab a highlighter. An important idea is coming up.

Let's start with one of the key rules of thumb in word of mouth. For every person to whom a happy customer talks:

- An unhappy customer tells five people.

- A formerly unhappy customer who is made happy tells ten people.

Think about this for a minute. Finding a way to make unhappy people happy is worth ten times more free word of mouth marketing than making them happy in the first place. It's probably a comment on the sad state of customer service these days that people are so surprised by being treated well that they run around telling everyone about it when it happens. But it's a great opportunity for you.

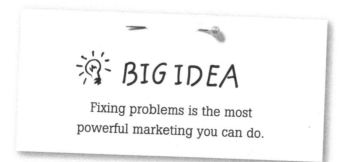

BIG IDEA

Fixing problems is the most powerful marketing you can do.

The shock of getting an acknowledgment that their concerns matter immediately converts detractors into powerful talkers. These new talkers will be out there telling everyone about what a great company you are.

Give your team the freedom to make these people happy.

Follow the lead of Ritz-Carlton Hotels, which enables any employee to spend up to $2,000 instantly to make a customer happy. The hotel knows that instant satisfaction results in long-term customer spending—and extraordinary gestures result in immediate word of mouth.

Can you think of another use of marketing money or staff time that gets such a payback in terms of free advertising or customer acquisition?

Bob Parsons, president of domain name registrar GoDaddy.com, did a great job of setting the permanent record straight. He and his company were taken to task by the blogs for opting to spend $2.4 million on an ad that would run during the 2005 Super Bowl. Marketing expert John Moore blogged his view that it was a bad idea. Within 24 hours, Moore's comments started getting picked up by other blogs and getting responses, most of which were very negative about the company.

> People want you to participate, as long as you do it as a normal person and not as a corporate spokesperson.

Instead of ignoring the online frenzy, however, Parsons replied the next day. He thanked people for their concerns and explained his reasons for going ahead with the ad—that the company had no debt and he was the sole investor; the money spent on the ad and the subsequent campaign would not take funding away from product development; and, as the founder, he really wanted to do it, even if it was silly. Throughout the following months, Parsons remained engaged, replying to others' comments and concerns.

His honesty and willingness to participate really struck people. Hundreds of comments were posted, most of which were positive. It is fascinating to follow the conversation and see how a little genuine participation turned people from attacking to publicly declaring their support for the company.

You have to take part.

In what is now considered a defining incident, the risks of not taking part became apparent when you consider what Dell did (or, more accurately, didn't do) in 2005 when it was criticized for poor customer service by Jeff Jarvis, a high-profile blogger. Jarvis posted some relatively mild complaints, and Dell didn't respond. The situation snowballed as more bloggers jumped on the story and piled on negative comments. The few replies that came from Dell's PR department seemed a bit clueless as to the significance of the situation. The bloggers persisted, daring the company to respond. By the time Dell did respond, it had lost significant credibility, and thousands of negative posts are still all over the web. The company had acted too late, and it paid a high price with a damaged permanent record and, undoubtedly, lost customers.

Case Study: Dell— Just Start Talking

Because Dell was one of the first companies to get called out for not listening to its word of mouth, it became one of the first companies to learn how to do it the right way. These days Dell has become known for its pioneering initiative in finding new ways to participate and connect with talkers—and respect for the company has increased directly as a result.

- The company blogs with a real human voice that makes it accessible and open—in English, Spanish, Chinese, Japanese, and Norwegian. Why Norwegian? Because a talented employee wanted to do it.

- Dell's 35 "Community Ambassadors" spend their days online talking, sharing, and solving problems. These folks are out on the front lines, building goodwill and finding new friends for the company. The program easily pays for itself by pre-empting or quickly resolving customer service problems.

- Dell has a Vice President of Community to make sure the company stays committed at the highest level and for the long term.

- Dell talks to its customers wherever they want to talk. The Dell crew jumps into any new community or technology that its customers decide to use.

- Anyone can suggest ideas for the company, comment on them, and vote for their favorites on Dell's public IdeaStorm site. Almost 10,000 ideas have been submitted, and more than 650,000 people have voted for them. That's a lot of customer love and support, just because the company asked.

When you look at these projects, they all started as simple websites, a little customer service time, and a lot of listening. Anyone can do it.

Dealing with Negative Word of Mouth

People will say bad things about you. In fact, it's already happening. So what do you do? The worst thing you can do is nothing.

If you've got a negative word of mouth problem, it's not going away by itself. People will keep talking, negative stories will keep spreading, and it will forever damage your reputation. If you don't get involved, it's going to get worse.

Probably the most common managerial objection I hear about word of mouth marketing is, "What if someone says something bad?" I hear all the time from skittish marketers and lawyers who are worried that if they start doing word of mouth, they will *cause* negative word of mouth.

Not participating because you're worried about negative word of mouth is like refusing to go to the doctor because you don't feel well. Participating in the word of mouth conversation doesn't cause negative feedback. It gives you the tools to deal with it.

The solution to negative word of mouth is more word of mouth marketing. In fact, many of the things you should be doing to manage negative word of mouth are the same steps you should already be taking to earn good word of mouth: getting out there, taking part, joining the conversation, and making new friends.

Negative word of mouth is an amazing opportunity. Don't forget: You get the most word of mouth from critics who become fans. Solving people's problems is the single best way to create loyal fans who will talk about you.

You Don't Need to Win

You can't have 100 percent positive word of mouth. (And you don't need it.)

Lots of people will say negative things, some justified, some not. You can't win every argument, you can't stop perpetual complainers, and some people will have legitimate issues.

That's okay—as long as far more people are saying positive things. In the end, it's the total conversation that matters. You want to work hard to make sure that most of what's said is positive, that you're responding as best as you can to the negative, and you're doing all you can to encourage your fans to support you.

Don't try to win every argument (you won't). Don't try to respond to every critic (you can't). Don't freak out over every little criticism (it just doesn't matter). Frankly, 100 percent positive comments are sort of suspicious. Nobody will believe it anyway.

Just show that you're working hard to make things better.

It's more important to be responsive than right.

The Four Defenses

1. Build Credibility Before You Need It

Let's say you find a bunch of bloggers attacking your products. You and your PR team could show up to post a perfectly worded response. Doesn't work. Why? Because you'll look like a shamelessly self-serving PR team that's only there to post a perfectly worded response.

Nobody knows you, and you're not a part of the discussion. Nobody has any reason to believe you over your critics who've been reading and writing in that community for years.

You need to be Norm, the guy from the TV show *Cheers* (where everybody knows your name). You need to be a regular participant, a known personality, and a familiar face in the room if you want any hope of responding to the negative word of mouth successfully.

If you do this well, you'll have a community that will ask questions and make suggestions instead of attacking. You'll have friends who will listen and who will defend you.

2. Bring It Inside the Tent

Where people complain is often more important than what they say. Most companies worry about negative comments on their own websites. That's backward. You are always better off if the criticism happens on your own website, blogs, and communities. Why?

- Your fans are there. A few critical posts will be drowned out by all of the happy customers talking.

- It's easier to respond on your own site than to chase comments spread across hundreds of sites.

- The positive responses will be right next to the original complaint, telling a complete story (instead of trying to respond to a post on one site with a response on a different site).

- If people can't complain on your site, they are more likely to complain elsewhere. You need a place to relieve the pressure.

3. Let Your Fans Do It

Sometimes the best way to respond to negative word of mouth is to ask your fans to do it for you.

If you did the rest of the stuff in this book right, your talkers are eager to help, and you have a means to communicate with them. Tell them you need help in a particular forum or on a particular topic. They'll respond. In fact, there's a good chance that they got there first and did it already. (Just be careful that your request for help doesn't look like an organized attack against the critic.)

After a while, your fans will start responding for you, without being asked.

A defense from your fans is always more credible than one from your employees.

4. Never Get Caught by Surprise

Conversations happen quickly online, and you need to respond the same day. When a bunch of people are talking about you in a lively discussion, there is no way for you to have meaningful impact if you aren't there at the beginning. If you show up a day later, the conversation is probably over and you missed your chance to influence it. If you find a complaint that is weeks old, the damage has been done, and it's probably too late to convert that critic into a happy customer.

How to Respond to Negative Word of Mouth

You should almost always respond to negative word of mouth. Some exceptions:

- A really small or obscure blog or message board where giving a response would actually give attention or credibility to something that no one saw in the first place

- An attack that is so obviously outrageous, rude, or nutso that everyone who reads it already knows that the writer has a personal problem

- A known attacker who is trying to provoke you to respond so he can attack more

Basic Response Strategy

1. *Respond calmly and offer to help.* Post a simple, reasonable response. Say you're sorry and offer to help fix the problem. Answer their questions, clarify confusion, show them how to get more answers. Provide a way for the critic to contact you.

2. *Do not get into a fight.* You will always lose. It's their website, full of their loyal readers, and they will get the last word. Responding should be done with good vibes and a good sense of humor. All you need to do is sound like a nice person who cares. Don't let anyone (including your boss) respond while angry.

3. *Be human.* Don't respond like a PR person, with a canned, corporate response. Respond like a regular person with a real name. It's easy to yell and scream at an anonymous corporation. But when someone shows up and says, "Hi, this is Jenny and I'm sorry for the trouble …"—everything changes. The critic feels embarrassed because suddenly he realizes that he was yelling at Jenny. Almost instantly, the anger goes out of the discussion, and you often get an apology.

4. *Write for the record.* In many ways, you're not really responding to the original critics. It's not entirely about them or their specific issues. You're writing your responses for every future reader. You want everyone to know that you saw a problem and tried to fix it. Everyone should be able to tell that you stepped up to do the right thing.

5. *Follow up.* Remember, now people are watching, so you need to follow up on the situation and deliver what you promised. A one-time visit isn't good enough. Keep coming back to make sure everyone is happy.

6. *Do something wonderful.* Every so often, do something amazingly nice for your critics. Replace a product with a huge upgrade. Send flowers. Mail a handwritten letter. Give a gift. Apologize to them (or thank them) publicly on your blog. Invite them over to meet your team. You'll have new best friends forever (and they'll tell everyone how cool you are).

Crackpots, Fake Reviews, and Stealth Competitors

Sooner or later, you'll run into someone who hates your guts. They attack, you offer to fix it, and the person keeps ripping you apart. Sometimes you'll find a competitor who is using fake identities to attack you.

Some people are just angry, mean, dishonest, or completely nuts.

That's okay. The important thing is that you're not.

Remember, people are smart. When future readers see those unfair posts that are making you upset, they'll understand. They'll know what's going on. They'll see the same ridiculousness that you do.

Just post a single, rational response—and move on. (This is really, really, really hard. But it's the right thing to do.) Learn to have a thick skin and a sense of humor. Channel your frustration into a positive direction: Get more fans to post more positive reviews, drowning out the negative.

One more tip: If the attack is posted on third-party websites, the site owners might help you. If you see something that is obviously inappropriate, ask to have it removed. They want clean, fair reviews and discussions as much as you do. Don't try to ask them to remove any legitimate negative criticism, but they will usually remove anything profane, abusive, or posted by a competitor with a fake user name.

Blogs Are Upside Down

When you're replying to negative word of mouth online, it's important to remember that blogs are displayed in reverse chronological order. How you end the story is what people see first in the permanent record.

The final word counts most. We read blogs in the opposite order from which they were written, and that's how they are archived. A raucous blogosphere debate may have lots of criticism of your company. But if you resolve it well and make the blogger happy in the end, that final entry shows up at the top of the blog.

Newer posts show up first in search results. This means that the current conversation is much more visible than what happened even a few days earlier. When you reach out and resolve an online problem, the positive resolution is the first thing seen by new readers.

You Always Win

In the end, negative feedback handled well is always a good thing. If you follow the advice in this section, you have a bunch of ways to win:

- *Love:* A critic becomes a fan who says, "I love these guys. They saw my problem, proactively came to me, and fixed it."

- *Respect:* A critic becomes a fan who says, "They couldn't fix my problem, but they saw it and tried to help. I respect them for it."

- *Truth:* Everyone now knows that an unfair attacker was unfair, and that you tried to do the right thing.

Every day you solve problems for customers, usually on the phone or by email. But these are private conversations between the customer and the service rep. When you solve a problem on the phone, nobody else knows.

When you do it online, in writing, it creates word of mouth. It's the same effort and the same cost on your end, but thousands more people see it. You benefit from the goodwill and from the saved costs of all those people who now won't need to call to find the answers to the same questions.

> Participating in word of mouth conversation doesn't cause negative feedback. It gives you the tools to deal with it.

So get out there and embrace the negative word of mouth. Start responding. You'll stop the negative, make new friends, earn new talkers, and generate a ton of respect.

TRACKING: WHAT ARE PEOPLE SAYING ABOUT YOU?

Your Job: Listen to the Word of Mouth and Learn from It

We all want to know when someone is talking about us. Now we can. When you track your word of mouth feedback, you can:

- Find out who the talkers are
- Learn which topics are working
- See if your tools are making a difference
- Join in the conversation

Above all, you can learn what people are saying about your company and your stuff so you can make it better.

Companies spend more than $7 billion each year on market research. That's a lot of money to find out what people are saying.

The clunky part of the research process is getting people to tell you what they are really thinking. We have tools to pull ideas out of people, and the results are often messy. Focus groups can tell you what people think, but those opinions are often limited to the artificial environment of the focus group itself. Surveys can provide useful information, but they depend on your asking the right questions.

Then, all of sudden, something really crazy happened.

Millions of people started writing down everything they were thinking. Just like that, people are blogging, sharing on social networks, and posting online reviews. And, as we know, much of that talk is about products and services.

So now we can just read it for ourselves. We don't have to hire companies to gather feedback for us. It turns out that the spontaneously written stuff on the web can be as useful as some of the formal research. Even better, what we find out on the web can be analyzed and used to project what people are saying in the offline world.

☀️ BIG IDEA

Word of mouth is more than marketing. It's also your best market research tool.

Advanced Word of Mouth Measurement Techniques

A new market research specialty is growing up around this phenomenon, devoted to measuring word of mouth. Major market research firms and dozens of startups are building an impressive science of word of mouth measurement. They can analyze the conversations about a topic, brand, or product with incredible precision and speed.

These companies can identify and understand who the talkers are, what they are talking about, and trends in the conversation. They can also examine your customer database and determine which of your existing customers are likely to be your biggest talkers, or they can go out and find new talkers for you.

I won't get into the details of these advanced techniques in this book, but you should know that they are available.

Simple Ways to Track What People Are Saying

I can't cram a full course on market research into this book, but I can help with some straightforward techniques that will give you a good intuitive sense of what people are saying about you, for little or no cost.

Now, as we know, most word of mouth is happening offline. That part of it is harder to track and measure. (Most marketers aren't invited into the bedroom or kitchen to listen in on personal conversations.) The online conversation, however, is very public and easy to study.

Use Online Tracking Tools

You can find a surprising amount of useful information with a simple search. In addition to showing you who's talking about you and what they're saying, these services can break down where the talkers are from, which sites they've come from, what they've looked at, what time of day they visited, and what they searched for to get there. They can also organize the data with handy charts and graphs.

Some search engines will also tell you just how influential each talker is. When you get a list of blog posts after searching, it also tells you how many people are linking to that blog. More links means more influence.

Encourage Feedback

Do you really want to hear what people are saying? Then make it clear that you are listening and make it easy to give feedback. The best way to understand the word of mouth conversation is to get people to talk directly to you. Here are some ways to do this:

- Put up a really simple, easy-to-find feedback form on your website, and reply to the people who use it.

- Create an online community or blog where customers and future customers can talk to you and to each other. This works great for building word of mouth credibility, because every post, good or bad, is publicly visible. It shows that you have nothing to hide.

- Ask for comments offline also. Put postage-paid comment cards in every package and by the cash register. Instruct your sales-people to remind people to give feedback, and tell them that you value what they say. Host a customer feedback meeting.

You'll get better results if you show that you care by putting the comments and your replies out in public. Print a selection of comments in your company newsletter. Post questions and answers on your website.

You can even create a system to specifically reward and recognize people for giving feedback. Amazon does it by labeling its most active participants as "Top 100" reviewers.

Listen to Tell-a-Friend Forms

Your tell-a-friend forms do more than just spread word of mouth. They're also a powerful tool for tracking the conversation. You know you have a hot topic when a bunch of people start sending referrals from the same page.

A good tell-a-friend form should send you a report every time it is used. That report will tell you quite a bit: what pages people are looking at when they feel motivated to tell a friend and how many people they are sending it to. The messages written by referrers are a great way to understand what people are saying to their friends about you. And although you should never send any email to the addresses entered into the form (that's spamming), you can track how many referred email addresses become customers.

You can get similarly good information from the comments on blogs, social networks, and online communities.

Measure Buzzworthiness

The problem with measuring page views on your website is that the pages that link directly from the home page are going to get more traffic. You know which pages are most seen, but not which ones will start word of mouth.

When you put a tell-a-friend form on every page, you get a very interesting ratio: number of referrals divided by number of page views. This is your "buzzworthiness" index, and it tells you which pages are the most word-of-mouth-worthy.

Move those items to the home page and highlight them for the rest of your talkers. You'll get more referrals and more sales.

Put Yourself Out There

There will be a lot more to listen to if people know you're involved and paying attention to them. When you go online, say who you are and ask for feedback. You'll be amazed at how easy it is to get people talking back to you.

GM has figured this out. Vice Chairman Bob Lutz has a blog—a good one. It's not GM propaganda. It's about cars, and Lutz is clearly a car guy. His genuine enthusiasm shows. The most interesting items are the comments posted after every piece.

The people posting on GM's blog pull no punches. The site gets hundreds of comments each week with lively interaction from people on the inside responding to real comments from the outside.

Although there are plenty of positive postings, some of it has to be difficult for Lutz and GM to read, but the value of this unsolicited, genuine feedback is incalculable. The conversation keeps going, giving participants huge amounts of information about GM and giving GM massive amounts of information about what customers think. The free research from the comments on the blog is worth as much as expensive research from focus groups.

As you get more active and involved, people will start to realize that your company is listening. They will start talking to you instead of about you. When that conversation gets good, then word of mouth and feedback start to accelerate.

Sharing of Direct Mail and Email

Direct mail is a useful tracking tool because the order forms usually have detailed codes that tell you who received each letter or catalog. Similarly, a good email server will track which email messages were opened by people who weren't on your original list. Use this information to start looking for people who place orders who were *not* the original recipients. These are word of mouth customers. The people who forwarded the offer are your talkers.

You can examine the trends in passed-along mailings to identify word of mouth patterns and new opportunities. Are you mailing to PR departments but getting orders from marketing managers? That shows there is clearly a word of mouth connection between the two departments.

Measure the Net Promoter Score

One very powerful, advanced measurement technique that you can use yourself is the Net Promoter Score, created by Fred Reichheld and discussed in his book *The Ultimate Question*. It starts with the fairly straightforward question, "Would you recommend this product to a friend?" Then it rates responses on a ten-point scale. This question works just as well for online or offline word of mouth.

If you subtract the percentage of negative responses from the percentage of positive ones (throwing out the neutral), you get your score. Basically, your word of mouth reputation is the number of people who respect you, less the number of people you annoy. To improve the score, you need to get fewer people saying negative things while earning more positive recommendations.

At company after company, a better score usually means better word of mouth and higher profitability.

Putting Value on Your Word of Mouth

By far the most common question I'm asked by big company executives is, "Can you put a specific value on word of mouth?" You can.

Unhide the Hidden Statistic

The first step is correctly identifying which customers are coming from word of mouth.

As I pointed out earlier, word of mouth has always been underreported—a hidden statistic—because most companies don't track it well. It's time to unearth it and give it its due.

Word of mouth needs to be clearly identified in your surveys and order forms. When you ask, "How did you hear about us?" be sure you're asking the right way. There should be a consistent, clear choice that indicates word of mouth. You won't be able to track the true impact of word of mouth if some say "from a friend" while others say "from a family member," "from a coworker," "from my doctor/lawyer/plumber/hairstylist," or "online." Tighten it up so that the answers are clear. "Online" might mean the banner ad you bought or a happy reviewer on a shopping site.

Do the same thing on your marketing reports—make sure there's a line for word of mouth there, too. When you list your sources of customers, be sure that word of mouth is properly reported alongside your other marketing campaigns.

Once you unhide this hidden statistic, you'll probably discover that you're getting a whole lot more word of mouth than you think.

Computing the Return on Investment of Word of Mouth

If you know the average lifetime value of your customers and you can estimate the number of customers you acquire through word of mouth, you can place a dollar value on your word of mouth marketing efforts.

This can also help you to put a value on your most active talkers. If you've identified who your best talkers are and know that they refer you to an average of six friends, and half of those people become customers, you can derive their value relative to customers who refer you to only two friends, and so on.

Here are some other ways to measure word of mouth revenue:

Referral Sales

Measure the value of sales generated by your direct mail and email forwarders, and you get a word of mouth value for each of them. You'll often find that people on your list who you thought weren't worth much because they never buy are actually generating significant revenue by passing along your promotions to other buyers.

In a study of the talkers in a local Chicago wine store, researchers watched a customer who was a classic talker. He had no affiliation with the store; he just loved wine and loved helping people. While he was shopping, he would go up to confused shoppers and help them pick out the right wine. The researchers measured whom he talked to and which wines were bought. The surprising result: This one talker generated more than $25,000 in annual sales for this single store.

Leads from Tell-a-Friend Forms

Every time someone uses a tell-a-friend form, you get a lead without paying for it. Credit it the same dollar value you would have spent to get a lead from any online ad. Actually, it's probably worth more because the word of mouth referral includes a personal endorsement and is likely to convert at a higher rate.

Sales Created by Customer Service

If you start to recognize customer service as not merely an expense but a way to create positive word of mouth, then you realize that spending on customer service generates a positive return on investment.

We know the cost of bad customer service when multiplied by the power of word of mouth. It's just as important to track the good side of the equation.

Find a way to follow which customer service moments are likely to generate a word of mouth referral (or even create an energized former critic who is now bringing in multiple referrals). Multiply these referrals by your average cost of acquiring a new customer. That's your formula for the value of great customer service.

Savings from Public Participation

Every time your team solves customer service problems on a public website, it reduces the number of people who call you to ask the same question. Estimate traffic to these pages to get a rough idea of how many calls were avoided and how much you saved because of it.

Ultimately, this kind of knowledge can help you make smarter decisions about where to invest money in marketing (and nonmarketing) programs that drive word of mouth. Putting a value on something is the best way to justify investment in it.

AND
IN THE
END...

Sixteen Sure-Thing, Must-Do, Awfully Easy Word of Mouth Marketing Techniques

Okay. You've read the book.

Now, before you forget it all, here's what you can do right now, today, to start a successful word of mouth campaign:

1. Look on the web for people talking about you.
2. Assign someone to join those conversations. Start today.
3. Create a blog.
4. Make a new rule: Ask "Is this buzzworthy?" in every meeting.
5. Come up with one buzzworthy topic. Keep it simple.
6. Put something by your front door that will remind people to talk to a friend.
7. Let your talkers sign up for a private newsletter.
8. Pick one easy way to track word of mouth.
9. Put a tell-a-friend form on every page of your website.
10. Put a special offer in an easily forwardable email.
11. Add a small gift and a word of mouth tool to every package you sell.
12. Have a private sale for your talkers.
13. Apologize for mistakes and solve problems fast.
14. Partner with a charity.
15. Do something unexpected.
16. Be nice.

And don't forget: ***Do something worth talking about!***

Creating Your Action Plan

Use the worksheet on the next page every time you get ready to plan a new word of mouth campaign. Work through each of the eight steps, and you'll have a plan that starts with easy and inexpensive actions and grows into a complete word of mouth program. It'll help you figure out your first steps—and then it'll help you think about the big picture. You can download more copies at *www.wordofmouthbook.com*.

Word of Mouth Action Plan

STEP	ACTIONS	YOUR PLAN
1. Assign a team	Who's in charge? Encourage participation	
2. Hit the WOM basics	Add sharing tools Multipliers	
3. Viralize everything	All docs sharable Move content external	
4. Start listening	Daily searches Track key voices	
5. Start talking	Participate Get an online service rep Blog Set up social media accounts	
6. Try lots of little things	One WOM project every week	
7. Go deep	Examine the fundamentals Are you buzzworthy? WOM philosophy across the company	
8. Have fun	Start launching crazy WOM stunts Reasons to talk!	

Download this worksheet at *www.wordofmouthbook.com*.

Choose To Be Good

Word of mouth marketing is about being good to people.

Real people will talk about you when they like you, your stuff, and the things that you do. The word of mouth that they create is far more powerful than all the advertising in the world. It's a wonderful thing: Happy people grow your business.

In the end, it's much more fun to go to work each day at a respected company that is honest, fun, and treats people well.

It's also a great way to become a successful business.

You can make that happen.

AFTERWORD

Yet Another Top Ten
by Guy Kawasaki

I just loved this book. (Word of mouth marketing is so Macintosh way-ish that I felt right at home reading it.) I've never written an afterword, but Seth did the foreword so this was all that was left for me to do.

Here are the ten ideas, stories, and recommendations that I liked most in this book:

1. Companies should hire a customer service rep to cruise the internet looking for kudos and complaints. When the rep finds kudos, he should thank the person. When the rep finds complaints, he should get the problem fixed.

2. Commerce Bank had a free change-counting machine in its branches that anyone could use. Beats the hell out of the machines in markets that take 7 percent.

3. A study showed that people who heard about a bad shopping experience are less likely to go to the same store than the person who actually had the bad experience.

4. The most powerful word of mouth advocates might be the customers who have done business with you only once so far. They are the most excited; repeat customers are probably used to the great product/service.

5. The Prostate Net contacted 50,000 barbers about talking to their clients about prostate cancer detection and prevention.

6. Incentives and rewards are likely to reduce word of mouth advertising because motivation becomes suspect. You can't "buy" word of mouth advertising.

7. The Wynn Las Vegas hotel gave free rooms to cabbies to generate word of mouth advertising via this very influential part of the transportation infrastructure.

8. The manufacturer of Duck Tape sponsors a contest for college scholarships called "Stuck at Prom."

9. A word of mouth campaign brought back Family Guy from the dead (that is, cancellation).

10. Zappos has a one-year, no-questions-asked return policy for shoes. This boggles my mind, although I've never seen my wife return anything to them.

Someday I hope to read about your kick-butt idea in a book like this!

Guy Kawasaki
blog.guykawasaki.com

THANK YOU

Everything I get credit for these days is really a synthesis of the generous work and clever ideas of hundreds of very smart people.

From 2004 to 2007, I had the good fortune to be the CEO of the Word of Mouth Marketing Association, where all these fantastic people were working to grow word of mouth marketing from a back-of-the-envelope casual practice into a real marketing profession. It gave me the opportunity to work side by side with some of the most brilliant marketers in the world, learning from them and innovating with them. I talked with them all day long, helped where I could, and absorbed neat, new things like a sponge. It's fun to be part of the birth of a movement.

From 2007 to the present, I've had the pleasure of working with an amazing crew at GasPedal. Our team is out there every day spreading the word about word of mouth. Their energy and creativity has brought so much help to so many companies. It's been a worthy mission, and we've had an impact far beyond our means. Our clients and the members of SocialMedia.org have been incredibly generous with their time, ideas, and resources. I'll always be grateful for their help and willingness to help each other.

My friend and colleague Peter Waldheim has spent more hours on the phone with me, helping me through both crises and craziness, than any rational person should, and I appreciate it more than I can express.

Cale Johnson, our editor, is one of the great voices in the word of mouth movement. His talent is what makes our big ideas such a pleasure to read.

And of course, Julie Grisham, my wife and love, has been unreasonably supportive and selfless through years of entrepreneurial ups and downs and personal insanity. I can only do what I do because of her generosity, tolerance, and understanding. (Plus, she's an amazingly talented editor who has put a huge amount of time into making this book better than I ever could have.)

Hi Charlie! Hi Ivy!

NOTES

NOTES

NOTES

NOTES

NOTES

NOTES

NOTES